ANTHOLOGY OF MEDIEVAL MUSIC

By the same author

Medieval Music

The Norton Introduction to Music History

Anthology of
MEDIEVAL MUSIC

RICHARD H. HOPPIN, EDITOR

Professor Emeritus, The Ohio State University

W · W · NORTON & COMPANY

New York · London

W. W. Norton & Company, Inc., 500 Fifth Avenue, New York, N.Y. 10110
W. W. Norton & Company Ltd., 37 Great Russell Street, London WC1B 3NU
Copyright © 1978 by W. W. Norton & Company,
Inc. All rights reserved. Published simultaneously in
Canada by George J. McLeod Limited, Toronto.
Printed in the United States of America.

Cover Photo Courtesy of the Newberry Library, Chicago
Library of Congress Cataloging in Publication Data
Main entry under title:
Anthology of medieval music.
  (Norton introduction to music history)
  Intended for use with the editor's Medieval music.
  Contains principally vocal music.
  1. Vocal music. 2. Sacred vocal music.
I. Hoppin, Richard H. II. Series.
M2.A5175   [M1495] [M1999]   784'.8'0902   78–9162
          ISBN 0 393 02202 1 (cloth)
          ISBN 0 393 09080 9 (paper)

                    5 6 7 8 9 0

Contents

Preface

This anthology was designed to accompany *Medieval Music,* the book I have written for the Norton Introduction to Music History series, and to provide the illustrative material thereto. The present book, therefore, includes neither description nor discussion of individual pieces. Even by itself, however, the collection should provide a useful and representative survey of medieval forms and styles from Gregorian chant through the rhythmically complex polyphony of the late fourteenth century.

As much as possible I have avoided reprinting pieces found in other, commonly available anthologies. I have also made it a point to include only complete pieces, with the complete texts of all strophic songs. The one exception is Perotin's four-voice setting of the Gradual for St. Stephen's Day (No. 35), for which I have given only the solo polyphony for the first word, *Sederunt,* followed by the choral plainchant that completes the first section of the Gradual. The decision to eliminate excerpts of longer pieces resulted, regrettably but unavoidably, in the omission of an important category of late medieval music—Mass movements of the fourteenth and fifteenth centuries. Even more than their length, however, the stylistic diversity to be found in French, English, and Italian settings of the texts of the Ordinary made adequate illustration of the repertory impossible within the confines of the present anthology. To leave these settings unrepresented seemed preferable to giving the misleading and even false impression of the genre that would inevitably result from the inclusion of only one or two examples.

Throughout the anthology, I have adopted the system of Latin syllabification used in the *Liber Usualis* and followed, more or less faithfully, in most scholarly editions of medieval and Renaissance music with Latin texts. The principles governing this system are relatively simple: 1) single consonants between vowels go with the following vowel; 2) groups of two or more consonants that begin Latin words, including those of Greek origin, also go with the following vowel; 3) compound words, including verbs with prefixes, must be divided into their component elements before further subdivision takes place. Although the system produces what may seem strange combinations of consonants at the beginning of syllables, e.g., *ct, gn, mn, ps,* and *pt,* it has the dual advantage of being familiar to singers and providing them with a greater number of syllables ending with a vowel.

Most of the music in the anthology has been newly transcribed, either from manuscript sources or, in the case of Gregorian chant, from the square notation of modern editions. (This notation is illustrated in No. 1.) Each of the other transcriptions follows the version of a single manuscript unless concordances provide corrections for obvious scribal errors. I have also retained the medieval spellings of my sources, again with the exception of the chant texts. What is presented here, therefore, is in no sense a "critical" edition. Instead, I have tried to indicate as accurately as possible in modern notation what medieval performers would have found in a particular manuscript source. In noting the sources of individual pieces, I have referred to published facsimiles when available, although in a few instances these are not the sources from which I took my version of the music and text. Concordances have been indicated only when there seemed to be some special reason for doing so. For most pieces, complete concordances can be found in the scholarly editions or manuscript inventories listed in the Chapter Bibliographies of *Medieval Music*.

The rhythmic interpretation of medieval music in unmeasured notation is both problematic and controversial. Four monophonic songs have been transcribed in triple meter (No. 4, melody 2, and Nos. 45, 48, and 49), and the same meter is suggested for No. 43 in small notes above the staffs. The polyphonic versus from St. Martial and Compostela (Nos. 30 and 32) have been written in measured but unmetered values that make all single notes and ligatures equal to a quarter note. Performances of both should be relatively free, however, with slight pauses at the ends of textual phrases. The nearly syllabic conductus No. 36 could not have been written in modal notation, but performance in a rhythmic mode was probably intended. The transcription is basically in the second mode, but the piece might be sung equally well in the fifth, with each syllable of text equal in value to a dotted quarter note. Measured values and regular meters in all other pieces are either clearly indicated or implied by modal notation in the original sources.

Something should be said concerning the translations included in the anthology. Those for biblical texts have been taken from the Authorized (King James) Version, although I have not hesitated to make alterations when the English and Latin meanings seemed too divergent. All but a few of the other translations are my own and are deliberately more literal than literary. Students and performers of vocal music need to know with reasonable precision what the text actually says. Few translations can duplicate the sense as well as the spirit and style of poetry or prose in another language, to say nothing of its sound. Yet recognition and appreciation of these qualities in a foreign language will begin to come when one knows the meanings of words and phrases and has at least some understanding of the grammatical construction. Within the limits imposed by English syntax and usage, then, I have tried to convey as much of this essential information as possible. If I have sometimes accepted a degree of awkwardness or inelegance in a translation in order to maintain a closer parallel with the original, I trust I have been neither inaccurate nor misleading in conveying at least the surface meanings of the texts. For the most part I have made no attempt to explain, or even comment on, hidden meanings and subtle implications that often make some texts seem impenetrably obscure. Many have biblical and other religious references; some are subject to symbolic or allegorical interpretations; still others refer to characters of classical mythology. Explication of all these aspects of the texts would necessarily have been lengthy, often conjectural, sometimes controversial. It has seemed best, therefore, to avoid commentary of any kind and to let the translations speak for themselves. May they do so with nearly the same clarity, or lack thereof, as the original texts!

Lest I be given too much credit as a linguist, I must acknowledge my great debt to colleagues and friends who have read my translations and corrected a number of errors. Professor Kenneth Abbott carefully checked both the translations of Latin texts and the texts themselves as they appear in various manuscripts and sometimes in modern editions. Professor Hans Keller went over the translations of troubadour and trouvère poetry, to which Professor Lowanne Jones gave a second reading before checking the other translations of French texts. Professor Albert Mancini corrected my efforts with medieval Italian, and Professor Aristobulo Pardo checked my first attempt at translating the Galician-Portuguese of the Cantiga de Santa Maria. For their many suggestions and improvements of my efforts I am deeply grateful. Responsibility for any remaining errors or infelicities of expression rests on me alone.

Special thanks must go to Edith Kimbell for her translations of the two songs by Neidhart von Reuenthal and to Stephen Kelly for his transcription of the caccia by Niccolò da Perugia. Their contributions saved me much time and effort at crucial moments in the preparation of this anthology. I must also acknowledge my great debt to William Melin for his help in checking transcriptions and preparing legible copies in the early stages of assembling material to be included. And finally, I again cannot say how much I owe to Claire Brook and her associates at W. W. Norton and Company, Inc., for their painstaking care and apparently inexhaustible good humor in dealing with the inconsistencies and idiosyncrasies of the material submitted to them. Their contributions to the quality of this publication can never be detailed, but they can and shall be acknowledged here with gratitude, affection, and esteem.

Richard H. Hoppin
Columbus, Ohio
November, 1977

List of Abbreviations

AR	*Antiphonale Sacrosanctae Romanae Ecclesiae* . . . (Rome, 1912 and later editions).
Ba	Bamberg, Staatl. Bibl., Lit. 115 (formerly Ed. IV. 6). Facsimile in P. Aubry, *Cent motets du XIIIᵉ siècle* (Paris, 1908; repr. 1964), Vol. I.
Beck M	J. Beck, ed., *Le Manuscrit du Roi* (Philadelphia, 1938), Vol. I (facsimile). Printed foliation (p.) not same as original (fol.).
CB	*Carmina Burana, PMMM* 9 (1967).
Ch	Chantilly, Musée Condé, 564 (formerly 1047).
Chic	Chicago, Newberry Library, MS 54. 1, fol. 10.
Cl	MS La Clayette (Paris, Bibl. Nat., nouv. acq. fr., 13521), *PMMM* 4 (1959).
DTÖ	*Denkmäler der Tonkunst in Österreich* 71 (Jg. 37/1), *Lieder von Neidhart (von Reuental)*, with facsimile.
F	Florence, Bibl. Medicea Laurenziana, *plut.* 29,1. *PMMM* 10 and 11 (n.d.).
Fauv	Paris, Bibl. Nat, fr. 146. Facsimile in *Le Roman de Fauvel,* ed. by P. Aubry (Paris, 1907).
FL	Florence, Bibl. Med. Laur., Palatino 87 (Squarcialupi).
LU	*The Liber Usualis with Introduction and Rubrics in English* (Tournai, 1952 and later editions).
Mach A	Paris, Bibl. Nat., fr. 1584.
Mach E	Paris, Bibl. Nat., fr. 9221.
MGG	*Die Musik in Geschichte und Gegenwart* (Kassel, 1949–68).
Mo	Montpellier, Faculté de Médecine, H 196. Facsimile in Y. Rokseth, *Polyphonies du XIIIᵉ siècle* (Paris, 1935), Vol. I.
Mod	Modena, Bibl. Estense, α M. 5, 24 (formerly lat. 568).
NPM	W. Apel, *The Notation of Polyphonic Music,* 5th ed. (Cambridge, 1961).
P₁	Paris, Bibl. Nat., lat. 3719.
P₂	Paris, Bibl. Nat., fr. 22543.
Pal M	*Paléographie musicale* (Solesmes, Tournai, or Berne, 1889–).
Pic	Paris, Bibl. Nat., Collection de Picardie 67, fol. 67.
PMMM	Publications of Medieval Music Manuscripts, Institute of Medieval Music (Brooklyn, 1957–).

Tu   Turin, Bibl. Reale, vari 42. Facsimile in A. Auda, *Les Motets wallons du manuscrit de Turin: Vari 42* (Brussels, 1953), Vol. I.

W_2 Wolfenbüttel, Herzog August-Bibl., 1099. Facsimile in *PMMM* 2.

Wag G   P. Wagner, *Die Gesänge der Jakobusliturgie zu Santiago de Compostela, aus dem sog. Codex Calixtinus* (Freiburg, 1931).

Worc   *The Worcester Fragments,* ed. L. Dittmer, Musicological Studies and Documents 2 (American Institute of Musicology, 1957).

1

HERMANNUS CONTRACTUS, *Alma Redemptoris Mater*

Antiphon to the Blessed Virgin Mary

Ant. 5.

AL- ma * Redemptóris Má- ter, quae pér- vi- a caéli pórta má- nes, Et stél- la má- ris, succúrre cadén- ti súrgere qui cú- rat pópu-lo : Tu quae genu-í- sti, natú- ra mi-rán- te, tú-um sánctum Ge-ni-tórem : Vír- go pri- us ac posté-ri-us, Gabri-é-lis ab ó-re súmens íllud Ave, * peccatórum mi-seré-re.

Fostering Mother of the Redeemer, who art the open door to heaven and star of the sea, come to the aid of the falling people who strive to rise again. Thou who gave birth, to the wonder of Nature, to thy holy Creator, virgin before and after, receiving from the mouth of Gabriel that "Ave," have mercy on sinners.

LU, p. 273.

2

Vota mea Domino reddam

Second Antiphon for Monday at Vespers, with Psalm 115 (116:10–19)

Vo-ta me-a Do-mi-no red-dam co-ram o-mni po-pu-lo e-jus. E u o u a e.

	Int. Tenor	Flex †	Mediant ‡
1.	Cre-di - di	propter quod	lo-cu-tus sum:
2.	E - go	dixi in ex - ces -	su me - o:
3.	Quid	re - tri - bu -	am Do-mi - no,
4.	Ca - licem	salu - ta - ris	ac-ci-pi - am:
5.	Vota mea Domino	reddam coram omni	po - pu-lo e - jus:
6.	O Domine	quia ego ser -	vus tu - us:
7.	Dirupisti. vincula mea:	tibi sacrificabo	ho - sti - am lau - dis,
8.	Vota mea Domino reddam in conspectu omnis		po - pu - li e - jus:
9.	Gloria	Pa - tri et	Fi - li - o,
10.	Sicut erat in	principio et nunc	et sem-per,

	Tenor	Termination §
(1)	*ego autem	humilia - tus sum ni - mis.
(2)	*Omnis	ho - mo men - dax.
(3)	*pro omnibus quae	retri - bu - it mi - hi?
(4)	*et nomen Domini	in - vo - ca - bo.
(5)	*pretiosa in conspectu Domini mors	san - cto - rum e - jus.
(6)	*ego servus tuus, et filius	an - cil - lae tu - ae.
(7)	*et nomen Domini	in - vo - ca - bo.
(8)	*in atriis domus Domini, in medio	tu - i Je - ru - sa - lem,
(9)	*et	Spiri - tu - i San - cto.
(10)	*et in saecula	saecu - lo - rum. A - men.

† The Flex is used only on the word *mea* in Verse 7.

‡ The Mediant has two accents, with an added note in anticipation of the second accent in dactylic cadences (´ ˘ ˘).

§ The Termination has one accent with two preparatory syllables.

LU, pp. 281 and 163.

Antiphon: I will pay my vows unto the Lord now in the presence of all his
people.

Psalm: 1. I believed, therefore have I spoken: I was greatly afflicted:

2. I said in my haste, all men are liars.

3. What shall I render unto the Lord for all his benefits toward me?

4. I will take the cup of salvation, and call upon the name of the
Lord.

5. I will pay my vows unto the Lord now in the presence of all his
people: Precious in the sight of the Lord is the death of his saints.

6. O Lord, truly I am thy servant; I am thy servant and the son of
thine handmaid.

7. Thou hast loosed my bonds: I will offer to thee the sacrifice of
thanksgiving, and will call upon the name of the Lord.

8. I will pay my vows unto the Lord now in the presence of all his
people, in the courts of the Lord's house, in the midst of thee, O
Jerusalem.

9. Glory be to the Father and to the Son and to the Holy Ghost. As
it was in the beginning, is now, and ever shall be, world without
end, Amen.

3

Christe Fili Dei and *Erue a framea*

Two Short Responsories: Sunday at Prime during the Year, and Passion and Palm Sunday at Terce

1. ℟ Christ, Son of the living God, *have mercy on us.
   ℣ Who sitteth on the right hand of the Father.
   ℣ Glory be to the Father, and to the Son, and to the Holy Ghost.
2. ℟ Deliver from the sword, *O God, my soul:
   ℣ And from the hand [power] of the dog my only one.

Psalm 21 (22):20

LU, pp. 229 and 239.

4

Aeterne rerum conditor

Hymn with Two Melodies

1. Ae - tér - ne ré - rum cón - di - tor, Nó -ctem di - ém - que qui ré - gis,
2. No - ctúr - na lux vi - án - ti - bus A nó - cte nó - ctem sé - gre - gans,
3. Hoc ex - ci - ta - tus Lu - ci - fer Sol - vit po - lum ca - li - gi - ne:
4. Hoc nau - ta vi - res col - li - git, Pon - ti - que mi - te - scunt fre - ta:
5. Sur - ga - mus er - go stre - nu - e: Gal - lus - ja - cen - tes ex - ci - tat,
6. Gal - lo ca - nen - te spes re - dit, Ae - gris sa - lus re - fun - di - tur,
7. Je - su, la - ban - tes re - spi - ce, Et nos vi - den - do cor - ri - ge:
8. Tu lux re - ful - ge sen - si - bus, Men - tis - que so - mnum dis - cu - te:
9. De - o Pa - tri sit glo - ri - a, E - jus - que so - li Fi - li - o,

1. Et tém - po - rum das tém - po - ra, Ut ál - le - ves fa - sti - di - um:
2. Prae - co di - é - i jam so - nat, Ju - bar - que so - lis é - vo - cat.
3. Hoc o - mnis er - ro - num co - hors Vi - am no - cen - di de - se - rit.
4. Hoc i - psa Pe - tra Ec - cle - si - ae, Ca - nen - te, cul - pam di - lu - it.
5. Et so - mno - len - tos in - cre - pat: Gal - lus ne - gan - tes ar - gu - it.
6. Mu - cro la - tro - nis con - di - tur, La - psis fi - des re - ver - ti - tur.
7. Si re - spi - cis, la - bes ca - dunt, Fle - tu - que cul - pa sol - vi - tur.
8. Te no - stra vox pri - mum so - net, Et vo - ta sol - va - mus ti - bi.
9. Cum Spi - ri - tu Pa - ra - cli - to, Nunc et per o - mne sae - cu - lum.

1. Eternal maker of all things, You who rule the night and day and give the seasons of the years to alleviate weariness,
2. By night a light to travellers marking off the night watches, the herald of the day (the cock) now sounds and calls forth the radiance of the sun.
3. The sun, awakened by this, unbinds the heavens from darkness; by this, the whole host of wanderers forsakes the path of wrongdoing.

Top line: *AR*, p. 6. Lower line: Gustave Reese, *Music in the Middle Ages* (New York, 1940), p. 105.

4. By this, the sailor recovers his strength and the waves of the sea grow calm; by this crowing, the Rock of the Church himself absolved his sin.
5. Let us arise briskly, therefore. The cock rouses those who are lying down and rebukes the somnolent. The cock denounces the nay-sayers.
6. By the cock's crowing, hope returns, health is restored to the sick, the sword of the thief is put away, the faith of the fallen returns.
7. Look on the wavering, Jesus, and correct us with a glance; if you regard us, our sins fall away and our guilt is washed away by tears.
8. Be a shining light to our senses and dispel the sleep of our minds (souls). Let our voice sing first of you, and may we discharge our vows to you.
9. To God the Father be the glory, and to his only Son, with the Holy Spirit now and through all ages.

5

Introit

for the Solemn Mass of Easter Day

I arose and am still with thee, alleluia: thou hast laid thy hand upon me, alleluia; thy knowledge is become wonderful, alleluia, alleluia. *Ps.* Lord, thou hast proved me, and known me: thou hast known my sitting down and my rising up. Glory be to the Father, and to the Son, and to the Holy Ghost. As it was in the beginning, is now, and ever shall be, world without end. Amen.

LU, p. 777.

6

Kyrie

for the Solemn Mass of Easter Day

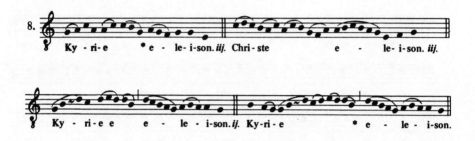

Lord have mercy. Christ have mercy. Lord have mercy.

7

Gloria

for the Solemn Mass of Easter Day

Gloria in excelsis Deo. Et in terra pax hominibus bonae voluntatis. Laudamus te. Benedicimus te. Adoramus te. Glorificamus te. Gratias agimus tibi propter magnam gloriam tuam. Domine Deus, Rex caelestis, Deus Pater omnipotens. Domine Fili unigenite Jesu Christe. Domine Deus, Agnus Dei, Filius Patris. Qui tollis peccata mundi, miserere nobis. Qui tollis peccata mundi, suscipe deprecationem nostram. Qui sedes ad dexteram Patris, miserere nobis. Quoniam tu solus sanctus. Tu solus Dominus. Tu solus Altissimus, Jesu Christe. Cum Sancto Spiritu, in Gloria Dei Patris. Amen.

Glory to God in the highest. And on earth peace to men of good will. We praise thee, we bless thee, we adore thee, we glorify thee. We give thee thanks for thy great glory. O Lord God, King of heaven, God the Father al-

LU, **p. 16.**

mighty. O Lord, the only begotten Son, Jesus Christ. O Lord God, Lamb of God, Son of the Father. Thou who takest away the sins of the world, have mercy on us. Thou who takest away the sins of the world, receive our prayer. Thou who sittest at the right hand of the Father, have mercy on us. For thou only art holy, thou only art Lord, thou only art most high, O Jesus Christ, with the Holy Ghost, in the glory of God the Father. Amen.

8

Collect

for the Solemn Mass of Easter Day

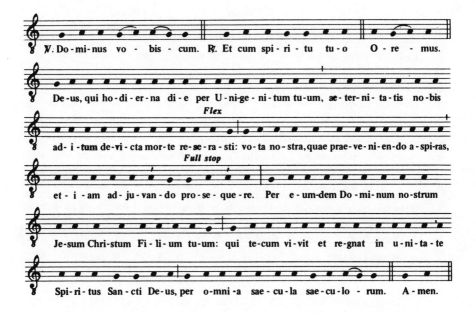

℣. Do‑mi‑nus vo‑bis‑cum. ℟. Et cum spi‑ri‑tu tu‑o   O‑re‑mus.

De‑us, qui ho‑di‑er‑na di‑e per U‑ni‑ge‑ni‑tum tu‑um, ae‑ter‑ni‑ta‑tis no‑bis

Flex

ad‑i‑tum de‑vi‑cta mor‑te re‑se‑ra‑sti: vo‑ta no‑stra, quae prae‑ve‑ni‑en‑do a‑spi‑ras,

Full stop

et‑i‑am ad‑ju‑van‑do pro‑se‑que‑re. Per e‑um‑dem Do‑mi‑num no‑strum

Je‑sum Chri‑stum Fi‑li‑um tu‑um: qui te‑cum vi‑vit et re‑gnat in u‑ni‑ta‑te

Spi‑ri‑tus San‑cti De‑us, per o‑mni‑a sae‑cu‑la sae‑cu‑lo‑rum.   A‑men.

℣. The Lord be with you. ℟. And with thy spirit. Let us pray. O God, who this day by thine only-begotten Son didst conquer death, opening unto us the gates of everlasting life; to the desires of our hearts which thou inspirest, do thou, by thy gracious help, enable us to attain. Through the same Jesus Christ, our Lord, thy Son, who with thee in the unity of the Holy Ghost lives and reigns God, world without end. Amen.

LU, pp. 778 and 100.

9

Epistle

for the Solemn Mass of Easter Day

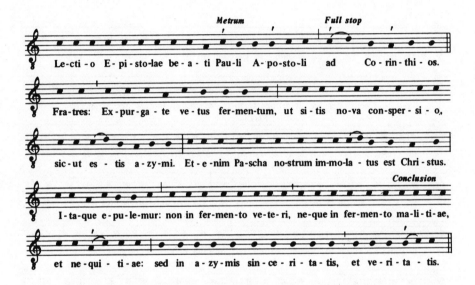

Reading of the Epistle of St. Paul the Apostle to the Corinthians. Brethren, purge out the old leaven, that you may be a new paste, as you are unleavened; for Christ our passover is sacrificed. Therefore let us feast, not with the old leaven, nor with the leaven of malice and wickedness, but with the unleavened bread of sincerity and truth. *(I Cor. 5:7–8)*

LU, pp. 778 and 104.

10

Gradual

for the Solemn Mass of Easter Day

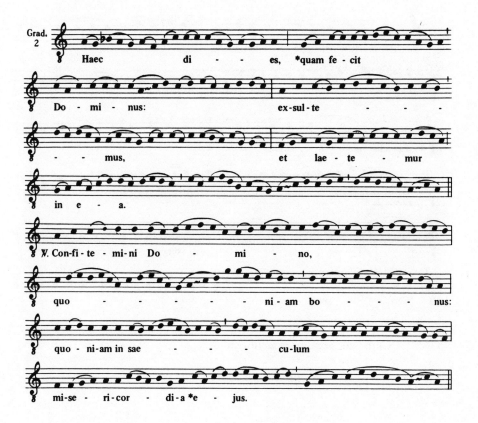

This is the day which the Lord hath made: let us be glad and rejoice therein.
℣. Give praise to the Lord, for he is good; for his mercy endureth forever.

11

Alleluia

for the Solemn Mass of Easter Day

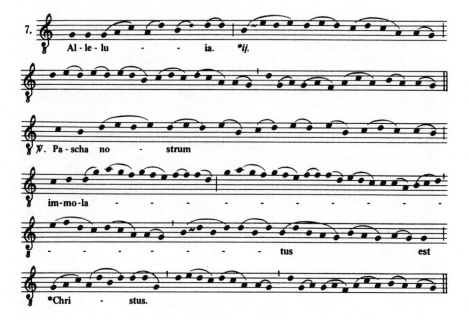

7. Al - le - lu - ia. *ij.

℣. Pa - scha no - strum

im - mo - la - - - - - - - - - tus est

*Chri - stus.

Christ our passover is sacrificed.

12

Sequence

for the Solemn Mass of Easter Day

Seq. 1. Vic-ti-mae pa-scha-li lau-des *im-mo-lent Chri-sti-a-ni.

2. A-gnus red-e-mit o-ves: Chri-stus in-no-cens Pa-tri re-con-ci-li-a-vit pec-ca-to-res.
3. Mors et vi-ta du-el-lo con-fli-xe-re mi-ran-do: dux vi-tae mor-tu-us, re-gnat vi-vus.

4. Dic no-bis Ma-ri-a, quid vi-di-sti in vi-a?
5. An-ge-li-cos te-stes, su-da-ri-um, et ve-stes.

Se-pul-crum Chri-sti vi-ven-tis, et glo-ri-am vi-di re-sur-gen-tis:
Sur-re-xit Chri-stus spes me-a: prae-ce-det su-os in Ga-li-lae-am.

[6. Cre-den-dum est ma-gis so-li Ma-ri-ae ve-ra-ci
7. Sci-mus Chri-stum sur-re-xis-se a mor-tu-is ve-re:

quam Ju-dae-o-rum tur-bae fal-la-ci.]
tu no-bis, vic-tor Rex, mi-se-re-re. A - men. Al-le-lu-ia.

1. To the Paschal Victim let Christians offer songs of praise.
2. The Lamb has redeemed the sheep. Sinless Christ has reconciled sinners to the Father.
3. Death and life have engaged in miraculous combat. The leader of life is slain, (yet) living he reigns.
4. Tell us, Mary, what you saw on the way? I saw the sepulchre of the living Christ and the glory of His rising;
5. The angelic witnesses, the shroud and vesture. Christ my hope is risen. He will go before his own into Galilee.
6. The truthful Mary alone is more to be believed than the deceitful crowd of Jews.
7. We know that Christ has truly risen from the dead. Thou conqueror and king, have mercy on us.

LU, p. 780.

13

Gospel

for the Solemn Mass of Easter Day

The Lord be with you. ℟. And with thy spirit. Continuation with the holy Gospel according to Mark. ℟. Glory to thee, O Lord. At that time, Mary Magdalene, and Mary the mother of James, and Salome bought spices, that they might come and anoint Jesus. And very early in the morning, the first day of the week, they came to the sepulchre, the sun being then risen: and they said one to another, Who shall roll us away the stone from the door of the sepulchre? And looking, they saw the stone was rolled away: for it was very great. And entering the sepulchre, they saw a young man sitting on the right side, clothed in a white robe, and they were astonished. He said to them: Be not affrighted; you seek Jesus of Nazareth, who was crucified; he is risen, he is not here; behold the place where they laid him. But go, tell his disciples, and Peter, that he goeth before you into Galilee: there you shall see him, as he told you.   *(Mark 16:1–7)*

14

Credo

for the Solemn Mass of Easter Day

18

Et a - scen - dit in cae - lum: se - det ad dex - te - ram Pa - tris.

Et i - te-rum ven-tu - rus est cum glo - ri - a ju - di - ca - re vi - vos

et mor-tu - os: cu-jus re-gni non e - rit fi - nis. Et in Spi - ri - tum San-ctum,

Do - mi - num, et vi - vi - fi - can - tem: qui ex Pa - trie Fi - li - o - que pro - ce - dit.

Qui cum Pa - tre et Fi - li - o si - mul ad - o - ra - tur et con - glo - ri - fi - ca - tur:

qui lo - cu - tus est per Pro - phe - tas. Et u - nam san - ctam ca - tho - li - cam

et a - po - sto - li - cam Ec - cle - si - am. Con - fi - te - or u - num ba - ptis - ma

in re - mis - si - o - nem pec - ca - to - rum. Et ex - spec - to re - sur - rec - ti - o - nem mor - tu - o - rum.

Et vi - tam ven - tu - ri sae - cu - li. A - - - men.

Do - mi - nus vo - bis - cum. ℞. Et cum spi - ri - tu tu - o. O - re - mus.

I believe in one God, Father almighty, maker of heaven and earth and of all things visible and invisible. And in one Lord Jesus Christ, the only-begotten Son of God, born of the Father before all ages. God of God, light of light, true God of true God. Begotten, not made, being of one substance with the Father, by whom all things were made. Who for us men and for our salvation came down from heaven. And was made incarnate by the Holy Ghost of the Virgin Mary, and was made man. And was crucified for us under Pontius Pilate. He suffered and was buried. And the third day he rose again according to the Scriptures. And ascended into heaven, and sitteth on the right hand of the Father. And he shall come again with glory to judge the quick and the dead; of whose kingdom there shall be no end. And in the Holy Ghost, Lord and giver of life, who proceedeth from the Father and the Son. Who, together with the Father and the Son, is worshiped and glorified; who spake by the prophets. And one holy, Catholic, and Apostolic Church. I acknowledge one baptism for the remission of sins. And I look for the resurrection of the dead, and the life of the world to come. Amen.

The Lord be with you. ℟. And with thy spirit. Let us pray.

15

Offertory

for the Solemn Mass of Easter Day

Ter - ra *tre - mu - it, et qui - e - vit, dum re - sur - ge - ret in ju - di - ci - o De - us, al - le - lu - ia,

The earth trembled and was still when God arose in judgment, alleluia.

LU, p. 781.

16

Preface

for the Solemn Mass of Easter Day

Per o-mni-a sae-cu-la sae-cu-lo-rum. ℟. A-men. ℣. Do-mi-nus vo-bis-cum.

℟. Et cum spi-ri-tu tu-o. ℣. Sur-sum cor-da. ℟. Ha-be-mus ad Do-mi-num.

℣. Gra-ti-as a-ga-mus Do-mi-no, De-o no-stro. ℟. Di-gnum et ju-stum est.

Ve-re di-gnum et ju-stum est, ae-quum et sa-lu-ta-re:

Te qui-dem, Do-mi-ne, o-mni tem-po-re, sed in hac po-tis-si-mum di-e

glo-ri-o-si-us prae-di-ca-re: cum Pa-scha no-strum im-mo-la-tus est Chri-stus.

I-pse e-nim ve-rus est A-gnus, qui ab-stu-lit pec-ca-ta mun-di.

Qui mor-tem no-stram mo-ri-en-do de-stru-xit et vi-tam re-sur-gen-do

re-pa-ra-vit. Et id-e-o cum An-ge-lis et Arch-an-ge-lis, cum Thro-nis

et Do-mi-na-ti-o-mni-bus cum-que o-mni mi-li-ti-a cae-le-stis ex-er-ci-tus

hy-mnum glo-ri-ae tu-ae ca-ni-mus, si-ne fi-ne di-cen-tes:

LU, pp. 8 and 109.

World without end, ℟ Amen. ℣ The Lord be with you. ℟ And with thy spirit. ℣ Lift up your hearts. ℟ We have lifted them up unto the Lord. ℣ Let us give thanks to the Lord our God. ℟ It is meet and just. It is truly meet and just, right and profitable to extol thee indeed at all times, O Lord, but chiefly with highest praise to magnify thee on this day when for us was sacrificed Christ our passover. For he is the true Lamb who has taken away the sins of the world; who by dying himself has destroyed our death; and by rising again has bestowed a new life on us. And therefore with the angels and archangels, with the thrones and dominations, and with all the array of the heavenly Host, we sing a hymn to thy glory and unceasingly repeat:

17

Sanctus

for the Solemn Mass of Easter Day

4. San - ctus, * San - ctus, San - ctus Do - mi - nus, De - us Sa - ba - oth.

Ple - ni sunt cae - li et ter - ra glo - ri - a tu - a.

Ho - san - na in ex - cel - sis. Be - ne - di - ctus qui ve - nit

in no - mi - ne Do - mi - ne. Ho - san - na in ex - cel - sis.

[Canon]

Per o - mni a sae - cu - la sae - cu - lo - rum. ℟. A - men.

Holy, holy, holy, Lord God of Hosts. The heavens and earth are full of thy
glory. Hosanna in the highest. Blessed is he who comes in the name of the
Lord. Hosanna in the highest. [Canon] World without end, ℟ Amen.

18

Pater noster

for the Solemn Mass of Easter Day

O - re - mus: Prae-ce-ptis sa - lu - ta - ri - bus mo-ni - ti, et di - vi - na

in-sti- tu - ti - o - ne for-ma-ti, au-de-mus di - ce - re: Pa-ter no-ster,

qui es in cae-lis: San-cti-fi-ce-tur no - men tu - um: Ad-ve-ni-at

re-gnum tu-um: Fi-at vo-lun-tas tu-a sic-ut in cae-lo, et in ter-ra.

Pa-nem no-strum co - ti - di - a-num da no-bis ho-di-e: Et di-mit-te

no-bis de-bi-ta no-stra, sic-ut et nos di-mit-ti-mus de-bi-to-ri-bus no-stris.

Et ne nos in-du-cas in ten-ta-ti-o - nem. ℟. Sed li-be-ra nos a ma-lo.

Per o-mni-a sae-cu-la sae-cu-lo-rum. ℟. A-men.

Pax Do - mi - ni sit sem-per vo-bis-cum. ℟. Et cum spi-ri-tu tu-o.

Let us pray. Thereto admonished by wholesome precepts, and in words taught us by God himself, we presume to say: Our Father, who art in heaven; hallowed be thy name: thy kingdom come: thy will be done on earth as it is in heaven. Give us this day our daily bread; and forgive us our trespasses as we forgive those who trespass against us. And lead us not into temptation. ℟ But deliver us from evil. World without end, ℟ Amen. The peace of the Lord be with you always. ℟ And with thy spirit.

LU, pp. 6 and 110.

19

Agnus Dei

for the Solemn Mass of Easter Day

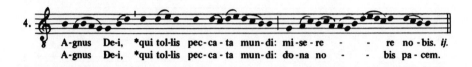

4.

A-gnus De-i, *qui tol-lis pec-ca-ta mun-di: mi-se-re - - re no-bis. *ij.*
A-gnus De-i, *qui tol-lis pec-ca-ta mun-di: do-na no - - bis pa-cem.

> Lamb of God, who takest away the sins of the world, have mercy on us.
> (*Twice.*)
> Lamb of God, who takest away the sins of the world, give us peace.

20

Communion

for the Solemn Mass of Easter Day

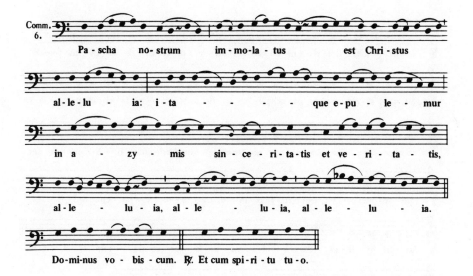

Christ our passover is sacrificed, alleluia: therefore let us feast with the unleavened bread of sincerity and truth, alleluia, alleluia, alleluia. The Lord be with you. ℟ And with thy spirit.

LU, p. 781.

21

Postcommunion

for the Solemn Mass of Easter Day

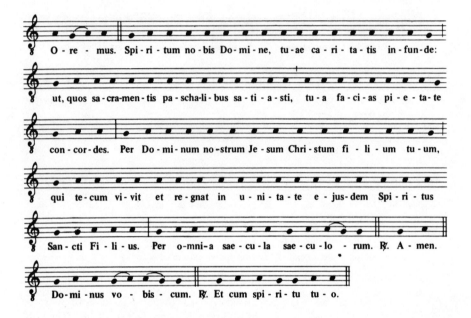

O - re - mus. Spi - ri - tum no - bis Do - mi - ne, tu - ae ca - ri - ta - tis in - fun - de:

ut, quos sa - cra - men - tis pa - scha-li - bus sa - ti - a - sti, tu - a fa - ci - as pi - e - ta - te

con - cor - des. Per Do - mi - num no -strum Je - sum Chri -stum fi - li - um tu - um,

qui te - cum vi - vit et re - gnat in u - ni - ta - te e - jus-dem Spi - ri - tus

San - cti Fi - li - us. Per o-mni-a sae - cu - la sae - cu - lo - rum. R̷. A - men.

Do - mi -nus vo - bis - cum. R̷. Et cum spi - ri - tu tu - o.

Let us pray. Impart to our souls, O Lord, the Spirit of thy love, that those whom thou hast fed with this Paschal mystery may be united in harmony by thy merciful goodness. Through Jesus Christ, our Lord, thy son, Son who with thee lives and reigns in the same unity of the Holy Ghost. World without end. R̷ Amen. The Lord be with you. R̷ And with thy spirit.

LU, pp. 782 and 100.

22

Ite, missa est

for the Solemn Mass of Easter Day

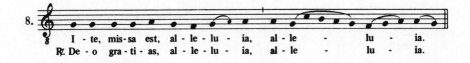

8.
I - te, mis-sa est, al - le - lu - ia, al - le - lu - ia.
℟. De - o gra - ti - as, al - le - lu - ia, al - le - lu - ia.

Go, the Mass has been said, alleluia, alleluia. ℟ Thanks be to God, alleluia, alleluia.

LU, p. 19.

23

Alleluia: Dicite in gentibus

Alleluia with Proses

Al-le-lu - ia

Pr. Lau-de-tur o - mnis ti-bi ca-ter-va ac cun-cti-po-tens

qui con-di-di-sti ce-lo-rum a-stra et re-gnas per - fe – cta.

℣. Di - ci-te in gen-ti - bus qui-a Do -

- mi-nus re-gna - - vit a li - gno.

Pr. Di - ci-te cho-ri cun-cti et psal-li-te in gen-ti - bus

qui-a ma-gna Do-mi-ni cle-men-ti-a su-is re-spi-ci-ens o-vi-bus re - gnant

o-mni-a sa-cra et im-pe-ra-vit a li-gno pro-pri-o fi-li-o su-o cru-ci-fi-xo

qui sur-re-xit et se-det in tro-ne De-i con-cul-ca-to Za-bu-lo.

Alleluia: prosula: Let all your flock be praised and You the all-powerful who established and governs the perfect stars of the heavens.

PalM XIII, 173 (fol. 87); *LU,* p. 801.

℣ : Say among the nations that the Lord has ruled from the cross. Prosula: Say, all choruses, and sing among the nations that, by the great goodness of the Lord regarding his sheep, all things sacred are supreme; and He ruled from the cross by His own crucified Son, who rose again and sits on the throne of God, having trampled the Devil under foot.*

---

* In texts such as this, which repeat as often as possible the vowels sung on the melismas, sound seems to take precedence over sense (and grammar). Although not indicated in the manuscript, the jubilus of the Alleluia should probably complete the verse, that is, before the second prosula, which adds a text to this concluding melisma.

24

Kyrie Deus genitor

Kyrie with Trope

Ky - ri - e - ley - son. De-us ge - ni-tor al - me Ky-ri - e

Sup-pli - ca - mus te o - mnes Ky-ri - e No-stra de-li - cta par - ce.

Chri - ste - ley - son Jhe -su Chri - ste red-emp -tor. Chri -ste

Be - ni - gnus no-bis ad-e -sto Chri - ste Ut sem-per lau-de-mus te di-gne.

Ky-ri - e Re-ple nos Spi-ri-tu Sanc - to Ky-ri - e De-us bo - ne sem-per

Ky - ri-e - ley - - son Quo ti - bi le-ti ca-na-mus e-ley-son.

God, fostering Father, We all beseech Thee, Spare our sins. Jesus Christ,
Redeemer, Aid us kindly That we may always praise Thee worthily. Fill us
with the Holy Spirit, God always good, By which we may with joy sing
eleyson to you.

PalM XV, fol. 277; *LU*, p. 62.

25

Eia Syon

Trope of Introit for Epiphany, *Ecce advenit*

E - ia Sy - on, gau - de et lae - ta - re a - spec - tu De - i
tu - i *Ec - ce ad - ve - nit do - mi - na-tor Do - mi - nus:*
cu - i ma-te - ri - es ce - li et ter - rae fa - mu - lan - tur
et re - gnum in ma - nu e - jus,
I - psi ma - net de - cus glo - ri - e at - que
ju - bi - la - ti - o et pot - e - stas et im - pe - ri - um.
Ps. De-us ju - di -ci -um tu-um re-gi da: et ju - sti - ti-am tu-am fi -li - o re - gis.
Glo-ri - a Pa - tri. E u o u a e.

Come, Syon, be glad and rejoice in the sight of thy God. *Behold, the king of kings is come,* To whom all substances of heaven and earth are servant, *And the kingdom is in his hand,* To him remains the splendor of glory and the jubilation, *and the power and the dominion.*
Ps. *Give the king thy judgment, O God, and thy righteousness unto the king's son.*

★ Sections with text in italics constitute the original Introit. The tone for the psalm differs somewhat from that in *LU,* p. 459.

PalM XV, fol. 31v; *LU,* p. 459.

26

Alleluia: Suscipe laus angelorum

Alleluia and Sequentia with Partial Text

Al - le - lu - ia.

Sus-ci -pe laus an -ge - lo-rum lau -dum car-mi -na le - ta
Pre-ce vo -to sup-pli - ci no -stra que mit-tit ca- ter - va.

Te con-lau-dans ad - o - rat san-cte rex in hac au - la
Et do -na per se - cu - la san-cta ta - ber - na -cu - la.

Receive, O praise of angels, the joyous songs of praise,
With prayer (and) suppliant vow, that our flock sends.
With great praises it worships you, holy king, in this hall,
and (your) gifts, holy tabernacles through the ages.

Paris, Bibl. Nat., lat. 1121, fol. 69v, and lat. 1136, fol. 95v.

27

Rex caeli

Sequence with Double Cursus

1. a. Rex cae - li, do - mi - ne ma - ris un - di - so - ni,
   b. Ti - ta - nis ni - ti - di squa - li - di -que so - li,

8. a. Mor - ta - lis o - cu - lus vi - det in fa - ci - e,
   b. Tu au - tem la - te - bras a - ni - mi per - a -gras.

2. a. Te hu - mi - les fa - mu - li mo - du - lis ve - ne - ran - do pi - is
   b. Se, ju - be - as, fla - gi -tant va - ri - is li - be - ra - re ma - lis.

9. a. So - no - ris fi - di - bus fa - mu - li ti - bi - met de - vo - ti*
   b. Da - vi - dis se - qui - mur hu - mi - lem re - gis pre - cum ho - sti - am.

3. a. Ci - tha - ra sa - pi - en - tis me - lo - di - a est†
   b. Ti - bi - met, ge - ni - tor, for - te pla - ci - ta;
   c. Cun - cta ca - ptus de - vo - to - rum lau - dum mu - ni - a
   d. No - stri quo - que su - me vo - ti har - mo - ni - am.

10. a. Hoc Sa - ul lu - di - cro mi - ti - ga - ve - rat, ‡
    b. Spi - ri - tu cum si - bi for - te de - bi - lem
    c. Spi - ri - ta - lem ab - o - le - bat ju - sti - ti - am,
    d. I - pso jo - co tu - a can-tans prae - co - ni - a.

4. a. Pla - ca - re, Do - mi - ne, no - stris ob - se - qui - is,§
   b. Quae no - cte fe - ri - mus, quo - que me - ri - di - e,

11. a. Haec si - bi cae - li - tus mu - ne - ra ve - ne - rant,
    b. Ut i - ram dul - ci - bus pre - me - ret mo - du - lis.

* The melody of 9 omits the first note. This fits the 15 syllables of 9a but leaves 9b with an extra syllable.

† Phrase 3a, with 12 syllables, has the melody of phrase 3b. It is here adjusted to correspond with the other 12-syllable lines.

‡ For phrases 10a and b, the last four notes are *F–F–D–E*.

§ The scribe omitted the penultimate note in the melody for 4a and b.

Adapted from J. Handschin, "Über Estampie und Sequenz," *Zeitschrift für Musikwissenschaft*, XII (1929/30), pp. 19–20.

5. a. Cri - mi - num   pur - ga ma - cu - las,
   b. Qui - bus cor - da no - stra he - be - tant,
   c. No - bis et,   bo - ne se - ni - or,
   d. Pro re - a - tu   do - na ve - ni - am.

12. a. Sic et haec   no - stra pla - ci - ta
    b. Ti - bi fi - ant, De - us, can - ti - ca,
    c. Et quod ma - la me - ri - ta ve - tant,
    d. Hoc fi - de - lis mens ob - ti - ne - at.

6. a. Nul - lus di - gnus tu - is pot - est ob - tu - ti - bus
   b. Prae - sen - ta - ri si - ne la - be fla - gi - ti - i,
   c. Ut lau - dem tu - o san - cto ca - nant   no - mi - ni,
   d. Et tu ge - sta non scru - ta - ris, pi - is - si - me,

13. a. Il - lum di - gnum fa - ci - e - bat re - li - gi - o
    b. Ac man - da - ta le - gis et ob - ser - va - ti - o,
    c. Nos   di - gnos tu - us a - mor et de - vo - ti - o,
    d. Fi - at fa - vor - que tu - us   nos   pro - se - quens,

[da capo]

7. Sed cor ho - mi - num.
14 Ju - vet dex - te - ra

15. a. Cae - lo - rum se - di - bus col - lo - cans a - ni - mas,
    b. Qui - bus hic lu - te - as de - dit in - du - ti - as

16. Car - nis no - strae.

1. King of heaven, Lord of the sounding sea, of the shining Titan sun and the gloomy earth,
2. Thy humble servants, worshiping thee with devout song as thou hast bidden, earnestly entreat thee to order them freed from their various ills.
3. The cithara is the song of the wise; to thee, Creator, may it be pleasing. Having obtained the whole service of praise of the devoted, receive also the harmony of our prayer.
4. May thou be appeased by our services, which we offer by night and also by day.
5. Purge the stains of the misdeed for which our hearts grow dull, and to us, good Lord, grant indulgence for our sins.
6. No worthy person can be presented to thy sight without the stain of sin; that they may sing songs of praise to thy holy name, thou dost not probe the deeds, most Blessed,
7. but the hearts of men.

8. The mortal eye sees the external form; thou, however, dost search through the hiding places of the soul.

9. With sounding strings, we servants devoted to thee attend the humble offering of the prayers of King David.

10. By this entertainment he had soothed Saul when from his soul, made feeble by chance, he was blotting out righteous justice; in this pastime singing your praises.

11. These gifts had come to him from heaven, that he might check anger with pleasant melodies.

12. And so may these our songs be pleasing to thee, O God, and because they check evils deserved, may the faithful soul gain by this.

13. Reverence and observing the mandates of the law made him worthy; let thy love and devotion make us worthy, and thy goodwill attending us,

14. May thy right hand assist,

15. placing souls in the seats of heaven to which He here gave the earthy garments

16. of our flesh.

28

Lament of Rachel from the Fleury Play *Slaughter of the Innocents*

Medieval Drama

*Then Rachel is brought in, and two consolers, and stand-
ing over the children she weeps, sometimes falling, saying:*

He - u! te - ne - ri par - tus la - ce - ros quos cer - ni - mus ar - tus!

He - u! dul - ces na - ti, so - la ra - bi - e ju - gu - la - ti!

He - u! quem nec pi - e - tas nec ve - stra co - er - cu - it e - tas!

He - u! ma - tres mi - se - re quae co - gi - mur i - sta vi - de - re!

He - u! quid nunc a - gi - mus cur non hec fa - cta su - bi - mus!

He - u! qui - a me - mo - res no - stro - que le - va - re do - lo - res!

Gau - di - a non pos - sunt, nam dul - ci - a pi - gno - ra de - sunt!

The Consolers support her as she falls, saying:

No - li, vir - go Ra - chel, no - li dul - cis - si - ma ma - ter,

Pro ne - ce par - vo - rum fle - tus re - ti - ne - re do - lo - rum. Si - que tri - sta - ris

ex - ul - ta - que la - cri - ma - ris. Nam - que tu - i na - ti vi - vunt su - per a - stra be - a - ti.

Facsimile in N. Greenberg, ed., *The Play of Herod* (New York, 1965), pp. 94–96.

Again Rachel laments:

He - u! He - u! He - u! Quo-mo-do gau - de - bo; dum mor-tu - a mem-bra vi - de - bo;

Dum sic com-mo-ta fu - e - re per vi - sce-ra to - ta? Me fa - ci - ent ve-re pu - e - ri

si - ne fi - ne do-lo-re O   do-lor! O   pa-trum!

mu-ta - ta-que   gau - di - a ma - trum Ad lu - gu-bres lu - ctus!

La - cri - ma - rum fun-di-te fle - tus, Ju-de-e flo-rem pa-tri - e la-cri-man-do do-lo-rem!

Again the Consolers:

Quid tu, vir - go, ma-ter Ra - chel, plo - rans for-mo-sa, cu - ius vul-tus Ja - cob

de - le - ctat? Ce - u so - ro - ris a - gni-cu-le lip - pi - tu-do e - um   ju-vat!

Ter - ge, ma-ter, flen - tes   o-cu-los. Quam te de - cent ge - na - rum ri-vu-li?

Then Rachel:

He - u, he - u, he - u! Quid me in - cu - sa - stis fle - tus in - cas-sum fu - dis - se.

Cum sim or - ba - ta na - to, pau-per - ta - tem me - am cu - ra - ret;

Qui non hos - ti - bus ce - de - ret an - gus - tos ter - mi - nos,

quos mi - chi Ja - cob ad - qui - si - vit, Qui - que sto - li - dis fra - tri - bus.

quos mul - tos, proh do - lor, ex - tu - lit es - set pro - fu - tu - rus?

Then the Consolers, raising the children, say:

Num - quid flen - dus est   i - ste, qui re - gnum pos - si - det   ce - le - ste,

Quid-que pre-œ fre - quen-tu mi-se-ris fra - tri-bus a-pud De-um au - xi - li - e - tur?

Then Rachel, falling on the children:

An - xi - a - tus est in me spi - ri - tus me - us; in   me tur - ba-tum est   cor me-um.

Then the Consolers lead Rachel away.

> *Then Rachel should be brought in, and two consolers, and standing over the children she weeps, sometimes falling, she says:*
>
> Alas! tender youths, what mangled limbs we see! Alas! sweet children, murdered by madness alone! Alas! whom neither piety nor your age restrained! Alas! wretched mothers, who are forced to see this! Alas! what now shall we do? Why do we not submit to these deeds? Alas! because joys cannot lighten our sorrows, we are mindful of the sweet pledges of love who are no more.
>
> *The consolers support her as she falls, saying:*
>
> Do not, pure Rachel, do not sweetest mother, hold back the tears of your grief for the murder of the little ones. But if you are sad about these things, rejoice at what you weep for; assuredly your children live blessed above the stars.
>
> *Again Rachel laments:*
>
> Alas, alas, alas! How shall I rejoice while I see these dead bodies; when my whole body is so troubled? Truly, the children will make me grieve forever. O sorrow! O joy of fathers and mothers changed to sorrowful mourning! Shed floods of tears, mourning the flower of Judea, the sorrow of the country.
>
> *Again the consolers:*
>
> Why do you weep, pure Rachel, lovely mother, in whose features Jacob delights? As if a bleary-eyed old wife of a sister could be pleasing to him.*
>
> Dry, mother, your flowing eyes. How do these rivers of your cheeks become you?

---

* This line apparently refers to Leah, Rachel's elder sister and Jacob's other wife. The interpretation of Notker's sequence (beginning *Quid tu virgo*) is difficult, and I have sometimes translated according to variant readings in other manuscripts. The biblical connection between Rachel and the slaughter of the innocents is tenuous indeed (Matt. 2:18), and Notker's text with its allegorical implications departs considerably from the story of Jacob and his two wives (Gen. 29–35. See also Jer. 31:15). Rachel now stands for the Christian *ecclesia* of the New Testament, which Notker also identifies as *virgo et mater*. Leah represents the synagogue of the Old Testament.

Then Rachel:
> Alas, alas, alas! Why do you reproach me for having shed tears in vain;
> When I am deprived of my son, who alone would care for my poverty;
> who would not yield to the enemies the hallowed bounds that Jacob
> acquired for me? To his dull brothers—how many, O sorrow, have I
> brought forth—he would have been useful.

Then the consolers, raising the children, say:
> Why must you weep for him who possesses a celestial kingdom? By
> frequent prayer to God, will he not help the wretched brothers?

Then Rachel, falling on the children:
> My spirit is anxious within me; my heart is troubled within me.

Then the consolers lead Rachel away.

29

Laude jocunda

**Beginning of Sequence to Saints Peter and Paul
(Melismatic Organum, School of St. Martial)**

1. a. Lau-de jo - cun - da Me-los, tur - ma, per - so - na
   b. Jun-gen - do ver - ba Sim-fo - ni - a rit - mi - ca

2. a. Con - cre - pans in - cli - ta Ar-mo - ni - a ve-ra
   b. Lu - ce qui au - re - a Il - lu - stra - re re-gna

Se - cli lu - mi - na 3. a. Ver-nant for-ti - a
Mun - di o - mni - a. b. Quo-rum me-ri - ta

Jam quo - rum tro-fe - a In ce - li re - gi - a
dis - sol - vunt cri - mi - na Hac di - e ful - gi - da.

* The second half of each versicle is written separately in the manuscript, with only the
  sequence melody in heighted neumes. Each repeat, therefore, should probably be of
  the tenor alone as a monophonic choral respond.

P_1, fol. 53.

1a. With joyful praise, assembly, sing forth the melody,

1b. joining words with rhythmic symphony.

2a. Resounding in the renowned true harmony, lights of the ages,

2b. who, with golden light, have illuminated all the kingdoms of the world.

3a. Whose mighty monuments now flourish in the kingdom of heaven,

3b. whose merits annul the faults, this shining day.

30

Omnis curet homo

Versus in Discant Style, School of St. Martial

O-mnis cu-ret ho-mo pro-me-re can-ti - ca Sunt com-ple-ta mo-do

di-cta pro-phe - ti - - - - ca.

(Refrain?) Est ver-bum ca-ro fa-ctum Vir-ga tu-lit flo - rem Stel-la ma-ris so - lem

In-cor-ru-pta no - vam Vir-go pa-rit pro - lem.

P_1, fol. 79v.

Quam mi - ran - da fu - it   gra - ti - a na - scen - - - - tis
Ut sic con - te - re - ret   vin - cu - la ser - pen - - - - tis.

Quo mor-ta - le ge-nus an - -te   te - ne - ba - - - - tur
Qui nos hic li - be-rat hic   be - ne - di - ca - - - - tur.

Let every man take care to pour forth songs; the prophetic sayings are now fulfilled. The Word is made flesh. A branch bears a flower; the star of the sea, a sun. The pure Virgin gives birth to a new offspring. How admirable was the grace of the child being born that so he might break the chains of the serpent by whom mankind was held before; He who here frees us, may we (here) be blessed.

31

Huic Jacobo

**Responsory for Matins in the Office of St. James,
with Melismatic Organum**

Hu - ic Ja - co - - - - - bo

con - do - lu - it Do - mi - nus tem - po - ris pas - si - o - nis su - e,

vel - ut ka - rus ka - ro su - o me - sti - ci - am car - nis su - e o - sten - dens

e - i et di - - - cens:

℣. Tri - stis est a -
Glo - ri - a Pa - tri

ni - ma me - a us - que
et Fi - li - o et Spi - ri - tu -

Codex Calixtinus, fol. 188. See *Wag G*, p. 72.

ad mor - - - tem.
i San - - - cto.* †O - sten-dens...

The Lord consoled this James at the time of His passion, like a lover to his beloved showing him the sorrow of His flesh and saying:

℣ My soul is sad unto death. Glory be to the Father and to the Son and to the Holy Spirit.

---

* The text of the *Gloria Patri*, which forms part of the monophonic chant, was added by a later hand beneath the polyphonic setting.

† The respond from *Ostendens* should follow both the verse and the *Gloria Patri*.

32

Nostra phalans

Versus in Discant Style for the Feast of St. James

No - stra pha-lans plau-dat le - ta Hac in di - e, qua ath - le - ta

Chri - sti gau - det si - ne me - ta Ja - co - bus in glo - ri - a,

An - ge - lo - rum in cu - ri - a.

Nostra phalans plaudat leta	Let our joyous company praise
hac in die, qua athleta	on this day, when the athlete
Christi gaudet sine meta,	of Christ rejoices without limit,
Jacobus in gloria,	James in glory,
Angelorum in curia.	in the court of the angels.
Quem Herodes decollavit	Whom Herod beheaded,
Et idcirco coronavit	and therefore Christ crowned
Illum Christus et ditavit	and endowed him
in celesti patria,	in the celestial dwelling-place,
Angelorum in curia.	in the court of the angels.

Codex Calixtinus, fol. 185. *Wag G,* p. 112; C. Parrish, *The Notation of Medieval Music* (New York, 1957), Pl. XXIII.

Cuius corpus tumulatur
Et a multis visitatur
et per illud eis datur

salus in Gallecia,
Angelorum in curia.

Ergo festum celebrantes
Eius melos decantantes
Persolvamus venerantes
Dulces laudes domino,
Angelorum in curia.

Whose body is buried
and visited by many,
and for this, salvation is given
them
in Galicia,
in the court of the angels.

Therefore, celebrating his feast,
discanting melodies,
venerating, we offer
sweet praises to the Lord,
in the court of the angels.

33

LEONIN (?), *Alleluia: Nativitas*

Notre Dame Organum with Substitute Clausulae

F, fol. 129. See *LU*, p. 1676A (*Alleluia: Solemnitas*). Substitute clausulae (S.C.): *F*, fol. 182.

lu -

ya

Jubilus

℣. Na -

S.C. (replaces mm. 55–68)

(ti-)   vi -

ti

vi -

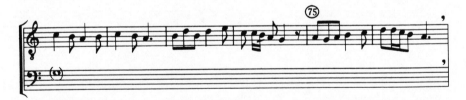

tas   glo - ri -   o -

se   vir -   gi -

nis

S.C. (expands mm. 95–101)

Ma -   ri -   e

Ma -   ri -   e

Ma -   ri -   e

ex   se -   mi -   ne

S.C.   (replaces mm. 134 – 148 or 154)

A -   bra -

A -

bra -

he   or -   ta

de

tri -

bu   Ju -

da,

cla-ra   ex stir - pe Da - - - - - - vid

Al -

le -   lu -

ya

Jubilus as above.

Alleluia: The birth of the glorious Virgin Mary, from the seed of Abraham, descended from the tribe of Judah, from the illustrious stock of David.

34

Ex semine

Clausulae

a.

Ex se -   mi - ne

b.

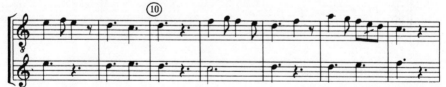

Ex se -   mi -   ne

a. *F*, fol. 176v.
b. *F*, fol. 168.

From the seed

---

* After the end of the repeated melody in m. 44, the note values in the tenor and its
  relation to the upper voice become equivocal. The transcription offered here is only
  one of several possible solutions.

35

PEROTIN, *Sederunt*

Organum Quadruplum (Gradual for St. Stephen's Day, Respond Only)

Organum: *F*, fol. 4. Chorus: *LU*, p. 416.

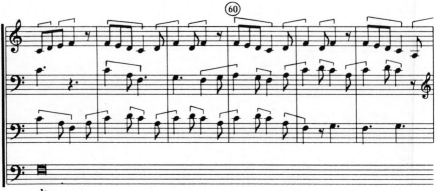

de -

runt.

The rulers were seated in council, and they spoke against me; and my enemies persecuted me.

36

Procurans odium

Notre Dame Conductus

Pro-cu - rans   o - di - um   Ef - fe - ctu   pro-pri - o

Vix de - tra - hen-ti - um   Gau-det   in - ten-ti - o.

Ne-xus est   cor-di - um   I-psa de - trac-ti - o   Si per con -

F, fol. 226; *CB* (text only), fol. 47v.

tra - ri - um   Ab ho - ste   ne - sci - o   Fit hic pro - vi - si - o

In hoc a - man-ti - um   Fe - lix con - di - ti - o.

Procurans odium	Averting ill will
Effectu proprio	by its own effect
Vix detrahentium	scarcely satisfies
Gaudet intentio.	the intent of detractors.
Nexus est cordium	The bond of hearts
Ipsa detractio.	is separation itself.
Si per contrarium	So, against the enemy
Ab hoste nescio	I do not know,
Fit hic provisio	this provision is made here,
In hoc amantium	happy condition
Felix conditio.	of lovers in this situation.
Insultus talium	The insults of such people
Prodesse sentio,	I feel to be useful;
Tollendi tedium	the occasion of relieving boredom
Fluxit occasio.	has passed.
Suspendit gaudium	Delay,
Pravo consilio,	by perverse intent,
Sed desiderium	holds joy in suspense
Auget dilatio.	but increases longing.
Tali remedio	By such a remedy,
De spinis hostium	from the thorns of enemies
Uvas vindemio.	I harvest grapes.

37

Soli nitorem

Notre Dame Conductus with Caudae

- lum.

I add brilliance to the sun, a handful of water to the sea, dew to spring water, I attach branches of fern to the oak when, to the leader who, by the illustrious star of his virtues, illumines the night and banishes the shadows of our age, I presume to subjoin an inscription of praise.

38

Ex semine Abrahe, Ex semine Rosa, Se j'ai amé, Hyer mein trespensis

Motet Texts Added to Perotin's Clausula *Ex semine*

Text 1: *a 2, F*, fol. 403v and *W₂*, fol. 146v (triplum omitted); *a 3, Worc* No. 81.
Texts 1 and 2: *Mo*, fol. 100v, *Ba*, fol. 15v.
Text 3: *a 2, W₂*, fol. 247; *a 3, W₂*, fol. 136.
Text 4: *a 2, W₂*, fol. 233v.

1. From the seed
   of Abraham, by divine
   direction,
   in the holy fire of your will,
   you bring forth, O Lord,
   the salvation of mankind
   from stark poverty,
   by the birth of a virgin
   from the tribe of Judah.
   Now you set forth an egg
   for a new birth;
   you will give fish and bread
   by this birth without a seed.

2. From the seed
   of a thorn, a rose springs up;
   fruit of the olive
   is plucked from the olive tree.
   A virgin is born
   from a descendant of Judea.
   The ray of the morning star

   shines forth
   from the darkness of a cloud;
   the sun from the ray of the star.
   A stone flows with honey;
   the flower of a maid gives birth
   to the Word, without seed.

3. If I have loved
   I should not be blamed for it
   if I am committed
   to the most courtly little thing
   in the city of Paris;
   but in all my life
   I have never had a pleasant look
       from her,
   To all but me she is
   frank and humble;
   but if she knew truly
   how I love her without deceit,
   she would take away my grief
   when she gave me her love.

4. Yesterday   morning,   deep   in
      thought,
   I wandered along my way,
   I saw beneath a pine
   a shepherdess, who was calling
   Robin with a pure heart.
   Soon I drew near her

and I asked for her love.
She replied at once:
"Good sir, I will not do it,
for I have a new friend,
and his love pleases me much,
I want no other than him.
With me you have failed."

39

Olim sudor Herculis

Monophonic Conductus in Sequence Form with Refrain

1a. O - - - - - lim su-dor Her - cu-lis mon-stra
1b. Hy - - - - - dra da-mno ca - pi-tum fa-cta

la-te con - te-rens, pe-stes or-bis au - fe-rens, cla-ris lon-ge
lo-cu-ple - ti-or, o-mni pe-ste se - vi-or, red-de-re sol-

ti - tu-lis e - ni - tu-it; sed tan-dem de-flo-ru-it
li - ci-tum non po-tu-it, quem pu-el - la do-mu-it.

fa-ma pri - us ce - le - bris ce-cis clau-sa te - ne-bris,
Iu-go ces - sit Ve - ne - ris vir, qui ma - ior su - pe-ris

Y - o - les il - le-ce - bris Al-ci - de ca-pti - va - to.
ce-lum tu-lit hu-me - ris At-lan - te fa-ti - ga - to.

Refrain

A - mor fa-me me-ri-tum de-flo - rat, A-mans tem-pus per-di-tum non plo - rat,

sed te-me-re dif-flu - e - ré sub Ve - ne-re la-bo - rat.

2a. Ca-co tri - stis ha - li-tus et flam-ma - rum vo - mi - tus
2b. Iu-go ces - sit te - ne-ro, so-mno qui le - ti-fe - ro

vel fu - ga Nes-so du - pli-ci non pro-fu - it; Ge - ry-on He-spe-ri-us
hor-ti cu-sto-dem di - vi-tis im - pli-cu - it. fron-tis A - che-lo-i-e

F, fol. 417, and *CB*, fol. 23v.

ia - ni - tor - que Sty - gi - us, u - ter - que for - ma tri - pli - ci   non ter - ru - it,
cor - nu de - dit Co - pi - e, a - pro, le - o - ne do - mi - tis   e - ni - tu - it,

quem ca - pti - vum te - nu - it   ri - su   pu - el - la sim - pli - ci.
Thra - ces e - quos im - bu - it   cru - en - ti ce - de ho - spi - tis.   *Amor* etc.

3a. An - te - i Ly - by - ci lu - ctam sus - ti - nu - it, Ca - sus so - phi - sti - ci
3b. Tan - tis flo - ru - e - rat la - bo - rum ti - tu - lis, quem blan - dis car - ce - rat

frau - des co - hi - bu - it, ca - de - re dum ve - tu - it;   sed qui sic
pu - el - la vin - cu - lis. Et dum lam - bit o - scu - lis,   ne - ctar huic

ex - pli - cu - it lu - cte no - do - sos ne - xus, vin - ci - tur et vin - ci - tur,
la - bel - lu - lis Ve - ne - re - um pro - pi - nat; vir   so - lu - tus o - ti - is

dum la - bi - tur   ma - gna Jo - vis so - bo - les ad Y - o - les am - ple - xus.
Ve - ne - re - is   la - bo - rum me - mo - ri - am et glo - ri - am in - cli - nat.   *Amor* etc.

4a. Sed   Al - ci - de for - ti - or   ag - gre - di - or   pu - gnam
4b. Dul - ces no - dos Ve - ne - ris   et car - ce - ris   blan - di

con - tra Ve - ne - rem. Ut   su - pe - rem hanc, fu - gi - o; in hoc e - nim
se - ras re - se - ro, de   ce - te - ro ad a - li - a dum tra - du - cor

pre - li - o   fu - gi - en - do for - ti - us et me - li - us pu - gna - tur,
stu - di - a.   O Ly - co - ri, va - le - as et vo - ve - as quod vo - vi:

sic - que Ve - nus vin - ci - tur: dum fu - gi - tur,   fu - ga - tur.
ab a - mo - re spi - ri - tum sol - li - ci - tum   re - mo - vi.   *Amor* etc.

1a. Once the sweat (labors) of Hercules—crushing monsters far and wide, removing the plagues of the world—shone afar with illustrious renown; but finally the former celebrated fame withered, cut off by dark shadows, when Alcides (Hercules) was captured by the charms of Iole.

1b. Hydra, made richer by the loss of heads and more savage than all other pests, could not make him anxious whom a girl tamed. The man yielded to the yoke of Venus who, greater than the gods above, bore heaven on his shoulders when Atlas tired.

(Refrain) *Love tarnishes the merit of glory. The lover does not regret time lost, but labors rashly to be dissolute in the power of Venus.*

2a. For Cacus, neither foul breath nor spewing flames were of any help, nor flight for false Nessus. Geryon of the West and the doorkeeper of the Styx, both triple forms, did not terrify him whom a girl held captive by an artless laugh.

2b. To the tender yoke he yielded who entangled in deadly sleep the keeper of the precious garden; he gave the horn of plenty from the brow of Achelous; by taming the boar and the lion, he won renown. He stained the Thracian horses with the bloody massacre of his host.

3a. He withstood the combat with Antaeus the Libyan. He countered the trickery of a subtle fall until he could prevent the falls; but he who thus unraveled the knotty embrace of combat was conquered, and conquered when he, the great descendant of Jove, slipped into the embrace of Iole.

3b. By so many reports of his labors was he distinguished whom a girl imprisoned with delightful chains; and while he embraces with kisses, she serves him the nectar of Venus from her dear lips. The man loosened by the idleness of Venus abases the memory and glory of his labors.

4a. But, stronger than Hercules, I undertake the fight against Venus. That I may overcome her, I flee; for this battle is more bravely and better fought by flight. Thus Venus is conquered: when she is shunned, she can be eluded.

4b. The sweet bonds of Venus and the bars of the alluring prison I unlock. For the rest, while I am drawn to other endeavors, O Lycoris, farewell, and may you vow what I have vowed. I have set the troubled spirit free from love.

40

Sic mea fata

Latin Love Song

1. Sic me - a fa - ta ca - nen - do so - lor, ut ne - ce pro - xi - ma fa - cit o - lor.
Blan - dus he - ret me - o cor - de do - lor, ro - se - us ef - fu - git o - re co - lor.

2. Fe - li - ci - ta - te Jo - vem su - pe - ro, si me di - gne - tur, quam de - si - de - ro,
Si su - a la - bra se - mel no - ve - ro; u - na cum il - la si dor - mi - e - ro,

(1.) cu - ra cre - scen - te, la - bo - re vi - gen - te, vi - go - re la - ben - te

(2.) mor - tem sub - i - re, pla - cen - ter ob - i - re vi - tam - que fi - ni - re

(1.) mi - ser mo - ri - or; tam ma - le pe - cto - ra mul - tat a - mor.

(2.) sta - tim po - te - ro, tan - ta si gau - di - a non ru - pe - ro.

(1.) A mo - ri - or, a mo - ri - or, a mo - ri - or, dum, quod a - mem, co - gor et non a - mor!

(2.) A po - te - ro, a po - te - ro, a po - te - ro, pri - ma si gau - di - a con - ce - pe - ro!

1. By singing I ease my fate as does the swan near death. An agreeable sorrow clings to my heart, the rosy color has fled from my face. From increasing care, lively pain, and declining vigor, miserably I die, so badly does love punish my breast. Ah, I die, ah, I die, ah, I die, because I must love and am not loved.

2. From happiness I would conquer Jove, if she whom I long for would deem me worthy. If I know her lips just once, once sleep with her, to face death, to depart gladly, and to end my life I'll at once be able. If I have not exhausted so many joys, ah, I could, ah, I could, ah, I could if I shall have received the first joys.

*P*₁, fol. 88, and *CB*, fol. 82.

41

JAUFRE RUDEL, *Quan lo rius de la fontana*

Troubadour Vers

Quan lo rius de la fon - ta - na

S'es - clar - zis, si cum far sol,

E par la flors ai - glen - ti - na,

E·l ros - sin - ho - letz el ram

Volf e re - franh ez a - pla - na

Son dous chan - tar et a - fi - na,

Dreitz es qu'ieu lo mieu re - fran - ha

1. Quan lo rius de la fontana
   S'esclarzis, si cum far sol,
   E par la flors aiglentina

   E·l rossinholetz el ram
   Volf e refranh ez aplana
   Son dous chantar et afina,
   Dreitz es qu'ieu lo mieu re-
   franha.

When the flow of the fountain
clears, as the sun will do,
and the flower of the eglantine appears;
and the nightingale on the branch
turns and repeats and refines
his sweet song of love,
it is right that I should take up my
refrain.

P₂, fol. 63v. Facsimile in J. Beck, *La musique des troubadours* (Paris, n.d.), Pl. VII (p. 65).

2. Amors de terra lonhdana,
   Per vos totz lo cors mi dol;

   E non puesc trobar mezina
   Si non au vostre reclam
   Ab atraich d'amor doussana
   Dinz vergier o sotz cortina
   Ab dezirada companha.

O love of a distant land,
because of you my whole heart
   aches.
And I can find no balm
but in your call
   with its lure of sweet love
in an orchard or behind curtains
   with the desired companion.

3. Pus totz jorns m'en falh aizina,
   No•m meravilh s'ieu n'aflam,
   Quar anc genser crestiana

   Non fo, ni Dieus non la vol,
   Juzeva ni Sarrazina;
   Ben es selh pagutz de mana,
   Qui ren de s'amor guazanha!

As I always lack this ease,
it is no wonder that I am aflame;
for there is no more beautiful
   Christian girl—
never will God wish it—
nor Jewess nor Saracen.
He is well paid
Who wins a bit of her love.

4. De dezir mos cors no fina

   Vas selha ren qu'ieu pus am;
   E cre que volers m'enguana
   Si cobezeza la•m tol;
   Que pus es ponhens qu'espina
   La dolors que ab joi sana;
   Don ja non vuelh qu'om m'en
   planha.

With desire my heart keeps yearn-
   ing
for her whom I love most;
and I fear that wish may cheat me,
if lust should take her from me.
For more prickly than the thorn
is the pain that is cured by joy.
Therefore, I never want anyone to
   pity me.

5. [Tornada]
   Senes breu de parguamina
   Tramet lo vers, que chantam
   En plana lengua romana,
   A•n Hugo Bru per Filhol;
   Bo•m sap, quar gens Peitavina,

   De Berri e de Guïana
   S'esgau per lui e Bretanha.

Without letter of parchment,
I send this vers that we sing
in plain Romance tongue
to Sir Hugo Brun by Filhol.
I know he is good, for the people
   of Poitou,
of Berry, and of Guyenne
rejoice in him, as does Brittany.

42

BERNART DE VENTADORN, *Non es meravelha s'eu chan*

Troubadour Vers

Non' es me - ra - vel' - ha s'eu chan'

Mielhs' de nulh' au' - tre chan - ta - dor,'

Que plus' mi tra·l cors' ves a - mor'

E mielhs' sui faitz' a son' co - man.'

Cor' e cors' e sa - ber' e sen'

E fors'' e po - der' hi ai mes:'

Si·m ti' - ra ves a - mor' lo fres'

Que ves au' - tra part' no m'a - ten!'

1. Nón ĕs mĕrăvélhă s'eŭ chán
   Miélhs dĕ núlh áutrĕ chăntădór,
   Quĕ plus mi trá·l córs vĕs ămor

   Ĕ miélhs sŭi fáitz ă són cŏmán.

It is no wonder that I sing
better than any other singer,
for my heart draws me more to love,

and I am better made for his command.

Beck M, p. 182 (fol. 191).

Cór ĕ córs ĕ săbér ĕ sén

Ĕ fórs' ĕ pŏdér hĭ ái mes;

Sĭ•m tírǎ vĕs ămór lŏ fres
Que vĕs áutrǎ párt nŏ m'áten.

2. Ben es mortz qui d'amor non sen
Al cor qualque doussa sabor;
E que val vivre ses amor

Mas per eneug far a la gen?
Ja Dombredieus no•m azir tan
Qu'ieu ja pueis viva jorn ni mes,
Pus que d'eneug serai repres
Ni d'amor non aurai talan.

3. Per bona fe e ses enjan
Am la plus belha e la melhor;
Del cor sospir e dels huelhs plor,
Quar trop l'am, per que hi ai dan.
Ieu que•n puesc mais? S'amor mi pren,
E las carcers en que m'a mes

No pot claus obrir mas merces,
E de merce no i trop nien.

4. Aquést' amórs me fiér tăn gen
Al cór d'ună dóussă sabór!

Cén vĕtz múer lŏ jórn dĕ dŏlór

Ĕ rĕviu dĕ jóy áutrăs cén.

Bén es mŏs máls dĕ bél sĕmblán
Que máis vál mŏs máls qu'áutrĕ bés;
Ĕ pŭs mŏs máls aĭtám bós m'és,

Mós er•lŏ bés áprés l'ăfán.

Heart and body and knowledge and sense

and strength and will I have given to him.

The reins so draw me toward love
that I can look nowhere else.

He is indeed dead who does not feel
some sweet savor of love.
And of what use is it to live without love

except to annoy people?
May the Lord God not hate me so
that I live one day or less

after I become such a bore
and no longer desire to love.

In good faith and without deceit
I love the most beautiful and best.
I sign from the heart and weep from the eyes,
for I love so much her from whom I have pain.
But what can I do if Love has seized me,
and the prison in which he has put me

no key can open except pity.
And of pity I get less than nothing.

This love so gently
wounds my heart with a sweet savor.

A hundred times a day I die of grief,

and I revive from joy another hundred.

Indeed, my pain is beautiful,
and my pain is worth more than other pleasures:
and because my pain is such a pleasure to me,

how great will be the pleasure after the suffering.

5. Ai Dieus! car si fosson trian
   D'entrels fals li fin amador,
   E·l lauzengier e·l trichador
   Portesson corns el fron denan.
   Tot l'aur del mon e tot l'argen

   Hi volgr' aver dat, s'ieu l'agues,

   Sol que ma dona conogues
   Aissi cum ieu l'am finamen.

6. Quant ieu la vey, be m'es par-
      ven
   Als huelhs, al vis, a la color

   Quar aissi tremple de paor
   Cum fa la fuleha contra·l ven.
   Non ai de sen per un enfan,
   Aissi sui d'amor entrepres;
   E d'ome qu'es aissi conques,
   Pot dompna aver almorna gran.

7. Bona donna, re no·us deman
   Mas que·m prendatz per ser-
      vidor,
   Qu'ie·us servirai cum bo sen-
      hor,
   Cossi que del guazardon m'an.
   Ve·us m'al vostre coman-
      damen,
   Francx cors humils, gais e cor-
      tes;
   Ors ni leos non etz vos ges,
   Que·maucizatz, s'a vos mi ren.

   [*Tornada*]
   A mon Cortes, lai ont yhl es,

   Tramet lo vers e ja no·l pes

   Quar n'ai estan tan longamen.

Ah, God! if we could distinguish
between the false and true lover.
If slanderers and deceivers
wore horns on their foreheads.
All the gold in the world and all
   the silver
I should like to have given—if I
   had it—
so that my lady might know
how purely I love her.

When I see her, you can tell it

by my eyes, my face, and my
   color;
for I tremble with fear
as does a leaf in the wind.
I do not have the sense of a child,
so seized I am by love.
And of a man so conquered,
may a lady have great pity.

Good lady, I ask only
that you take me as a servitor,

for I will serve you as my good
   lord,
whatever wages I may get.
You see me at your command,

noble gentle heart, gay and courteous.
You are not a bear or a lion
who would kill me if I surrender
   myself to you.

To my Courtly One, there where
   she is,
I send this vers, and may she not
   be angry
because I have been away so long.

43

MARCABRU, *L'autrier jost' una sebissa*

Troubadour Pastorela

L'au - trier jost' u - na se - bis - sa

Tro - bei pas - to - ra mes - tis - sa,

De joi e de sen mas - sis - sa,

E fon fil - ha de vi - la - na,

Cap' e go - nel' e pe - lis - sa

Vest e ca - mi - za tres - lis - sa,

Sot - lars e caus - sas de la - na.

1. L'autrier jost' una sebissa
   Trobei pastora mestissa,
   De joi e de sen massissa.
   E fon filha de vilana,

The other day by a hedge-row
I found a lowly shepherdess,
full of joy and good sense.
She was the daughter of a country
woman,

P₂, fol. 5v. Facsimile in R. Monterosso, *Musica e ritmica de Trovatori* (Milan, 1956), facing p. 48.

Cap' e gonel' e pelissa
Vest e camiza treslissa,
Sotlars e caussas de lana.

wearing hood and cloak and gown
and a very rough blouse,
with heavy shoes and woolen
    stockings.

2. Vers leis vinc per la planissa:
"Toza," fi•m eu, "res faitissa,
Dol ai gran del ven que•us
    fissa."
"Senher," so dis la vilana,
"Merce Deu e ma noirissa,

I came to her across the field:
"My dear," I said, "Pretty thing,
it pains me much that the wind
    should freeze you."
"My Lord," said the country girl,
"thanks be to God and to her who
    nursed me,

Pauc m'o pretz si•l vens
    m'erissa,
Qu'alegreta sui e sana."

I do not mind the wind that tan-
    gles my hair,
for I am joyous and healthy."

3. "Toza," fi•m eu, "cauza pia,

"My dear," I said, "object of re-
    spect,

Destoutz me sui de la via,
Per far a vos companhia;
Quar aitals toza vilana
No pot ses parelh paria
Pastorgar tanta bestia
En aital loc tan soldana."

I came out of my way
to keep you company;
for such a little country girl
should not be watching
so many cattle
in a place like this all alone."

4. "Don," fetz ela, "qui que•m
    sia,
Ben conosc sen e folia.
La vostra parelharia,
Senher," so dis la vilana,
"Lai on se tanh si s'estia

"Sir," she said, "whatever I may
    be,
I know wisdom from folly.
Your company,
my Lord," said the country girl,
"you should keep where it
    belongs.

Que tals la cui' en bailia

For when such as I thinks to
    possess a man,

Tener, no•n a mas l'ufana."

she has only the shadow."

5. "Toza de gentil afaire,
Cavaliers fon vostre paire
Que•us engenret en la maire,

"Girl of noble manners,
your father was surely a knight,
who engendered you in your
    mother,

Car fon corteza vilana,
Con plus vos gart, m'es be-
    laire,
E per vostre joi m'esclaire,
Si fossetz un pauc humana."

for she was a courtly peasant.
The more I look at you, the pret-
    tier you seem,
and I am lit by your joy,
if only you showed a bit of hu-
    manity."

6. "Don, tot mon linh e mon aire
Vei revertir e retraire
Al vezoig et a l'araire,
Senher," so dis la vilana;

"Sir, all my lineage
I see going back
to the sickle and the plow,
my lord," said the farm girl.

"Mas tals se fai cavalgaire

Qu'atrestal deuria faire
Los seis jorns de la setmana."

7. "Toza," fi•m eu, "gentils fada
Vos adastret, quan fos nada,
D'una beutat esmerada
Sobre tot' autra vilana:
E seria• us ben doblada

Si•m vezi' una vegada
Sobeira e vos sotrana."

8. "Senher, tan m'avetz lauzada,

Que tota'n sui enoida.
Pos en pretz m'avetz levada,

Senher," so dis la vilana,
"Per so•n auretz per soudada
Al partir 'bada, fol, bada!'
E la muz'a meliana."

9. "Toza," fel cor e salvatge
Adomesg'om per uzatge.
Ben conosc al trespassatge
Qu'ab aital toza vilana
Pot hom far ric companhatge

Ab amistat de coratge,
Quan l'us l'autre non engana."

10. "Don, hom coitatz de folatge

Jur' e pliu e promet gatge.

Si•m fariatz homenatge,
Senher," so dis la vilana;
"Mas ges per un pauc d'in-
tratge
No volh de mon piuzelatge

Camjar per nom de putana."

11. "Toza, tota creatura
Revertis a sa natura.
Parelhar parelhadura

Devem eu e vos, vilana.
A l'abric lonc la pastura:

"But some who call themselves
knights
would do better
to work six days of the week."

"My dear," I said, "a good fairy
endowed you at your birth
with a pure beauty
beyond all other peasant girls.
And you would be doubly beautiful
if I saw you once
beneath, with me above you."

"My lord, you have praised me so
much
that everyone would envy me.
Since you have driven up my
value,
my lord," said the peasant girl,
"you shall have this reward
in parting: 'Gape, fool, gape,'
and wait all afternoon."

"My dear, a wild and savage heart
can be tamed with usage.
I well know that by traveling
with such a peasant girl
a man can have a rich com-
panionship,
with heartfelt friendship,
if one does not deceive the other."

"Sir, a man in a moment of mad-
ness,
swears and pledges and promises a
gage.
So would you do me homage,
my lord," said the peasant girl.
"But for a small entrance fee,

I do not want to exchange my
maidenhood
for the name of a whore."

"My dear, every creature
reverts to its nature.
We should become a pair of
equals,
you and I, peasant girl,
in the shelter beside the pasture.

Que melhs n'estaretz segura
Per far la cauza doussana.

There you will be much safer
to do the sweet thing."

12. "Don, oc; mas segon dreitura
Cerca fols sa folatura,
Cortes cortez' aventura,

E•l vilas ab la vilana.
En tal loc fai sens fraitura
On hom non garda mezura,

Se ditz la gens anciana."

"Sir, yes; but it is right
that the fool seek his folly,
the man of court his courtly ad-
venture,
and the peasant his farm girl.
'Good sense is destroyed,
where a man does not keep the
measure,'
so say the old folk."

13. "Toza, de vostra figura
Non vi autra plus tafura
Ni de son cor plus trefana.

"My dear, I never saw another
with a more mischievous face
or a more treacherous heart."

14. "Don, lo cavecs vos ahura
Que tals bad'en la peintura
Qu'autre n'espera la mana.

"Sir, the owl warns you:
this one gapes at the painting,
another waits for manna."

44

Bele Doette

Chanson de Toile

1.	Be	-	le	Do - et - te	as	fe - nes	-	tres	se siet,
2.	Uns	es -	cui - ers as		de - grez	de	la	sa - le
3.	Be	-	le	Do - et - te	tan - tost	li	de -	man-da:
4.	Be	-	le	Do - et - te	s'est	en es	-	tant	dre - ci - e,
5.	Be	-	le	Do - et - te	li	prist a	de -	man-der:
6.	Be	-	le	Do - et - te	a	pris son	duel	a	fai - re:
7.	Por	vos	fe - rai	u - ne	ab	-	bai - e	te - le
8.	Be	-	le	Do - et - te	prist son	ab	-	baie	a fai - re,

(1.)	Lit	en	un	li	-	vre, mais	au cuer	ne l'en tient;
(2.)	Est	des -	sen - duz,		s'est	des - tros - sé,	sa ma - le.
(3.)	"Ou	est	mes si	-	res, que	ne vi	tel pie - ça?"
(4.)	Voit	l'es -	cui - er,		vers	lui s'est	a - dre - ci - e;
(5.)	"Ou	est	mes si	-	res, cui	je doi	tant a - mer?"
(6.)	"Tant	mar	i	fus	-	tes, cuens	Do, frans	de - bo - nai - re.
(7.)	Qant	iert	li	jors		que la	feste	iert no - me - ie,
(8.)	Qui	mout	est	gran	-	de, et	a - des	se - ra mai - re:

(1.)	De	son	a - mi	Do - on	li		re -	so - vient,
(2.)	Be	- le	Do - et - te	les de - grez	en	a - va - le
(3.)	Cil	ot	tel duel	que de pi	-	tié	plo - ra.
(4.)	En	son	cuer est	do - lante et		cor -	re - ci - e
(5.)	"En	non	Deu, da - me,	nel vos	quier	mais	ce - ler,
(6.)	Por	vos - tre a -	mor ves -	ti - rai	je	la	hai - re,
(7.)	Se	nus	i vient	qui ait s'a	-	mor	fau - se - ie,
(8.)	Toz	cels	et ce - les	vo - dra	de -	danz	a - trai - re

Le Chansonnier de Saint-Germain-des-Prés, ed. P. Meyer and G. Raynaud (Paris, 1892), fol. 66.

(1.) Q'en au - tres	ter -		res est a - lez	tor - noi - er.
(2.) Ne cui - de	pas		o - ir no -	vel - le ma - le.
(3.) Be - le Do - et	-	te main - te - nant	se pas - ma.
(4.) Por son sei - gnor		dont e - le	ne voit mi - e.
(5.) Morz est mes si	-	res, o - cis fu	au jos - ter."
(6.) Ne sor mon cors		n'a - vra pe - li - ce	vai - re.
(7.) Ja del mos - tier		ne sa - ve - ra l'en - tre - ie.
(8.) Qui por a - mor		se - vent peine et mal	trai- re.

(Por vos de - ven - rai   non - ne

Ref: *E   or   en   ai   dol.*
A   l'e - gli - se   Saint   Pol.") *

1. Lovely Doette sat at a window reading a book, but her heart was not in it; She recalled her friend Doon, who had gone tourneying in other lands. See now what grief I have.

2. A squire dismounted at the staircase of the hall and untied his saddlebags. Lovely Doette ran down the steps, not thinking to hear bad news. See now what grief I have.

3. Lovely Doette asked him at once: "Where is my lord whom I have not seen for so long?" The squire had such grief that he wept for pity. Then lovely Doette fainted away. See now what grief I have.

4. Standing again, lovely Doette sees the squire and addresses herself to him; in her heart she is sorrowful and afflicted for her lord whom she does not see. See now what grief I have.

5. Lovely Doette asked him: "Where is my lord whom I should love so much?" "In the name of God, lady, I shall no longer seek to hide anything from you. My lord is dead; he was killed in jousting." See now what grief I have.

6. Lovely Doette began to mourn. "Such sorrow was there, count Do, true noble man. For your love I shall wear a hair shirt, and on my body I shall not wear a fur cloak. See now what grief I have. For you I shall become a nun in the church of Saint Paul.

7. For you I shall build such an abbey that, on the day the feast is announced, if any comes who has deceived his love he will not be able to enter the church. See now what grief I have. For you I shall become a nun in the church of Saint Paul.

8. Lovely Doette began to build her abbey, which is very large, and now she will be the abbess. She will gather there all those (men and women) who for love have known pain and sorrow. See now what grief I have. For you I shall become a nun in the church of Saint Paul.

---

* Follows the usual refrain after stanzas 6–8.

45

JEHANS ERARS, *Au tems pascor*

Trouvère Pastourelle

Au tems pas-cor L'au-trier un jor Par un ries che-vau-choi - e,
En un des-tor Par la cha-lor Tro-vai em-mi ma voi - e

Per-rins et Gui-ot et Ro-gier; Iert la fes-te cri-é - e;
Entr'eux di-ent qu'a-pres man-gier Gui i men-ra po-gné - e

A la clo-chette et au fres-tel Fe - ra la ra - bar - di - e.
Et de sa muse au grant fo - rel

Ci - ba - la-la du riaus du riaus, Ci - ba - la-la du - ri - e.

1. Au tems pascor	At Easter time
L'autrier un jor	the other day,
Par un ries chevauchoie,	I was riding by a pasture.
En un destor	In a secluded spot
Par la chalor	because of the heat,
Trovai emmi ma voie	I found in my way
Perrins et Guiot et Rogier;	Perrin and Guiot and Rogier.
Entr' eux dient qu'apres mangier	Among themselves they said that after eating
Iert la feste criée;	a fete would be announced.
Gui i menra pognée	Gui will lead the tumult,
A la clochette et au frestel	with bell and panpipes
Et de sa muse au grant forel	and his bagpipe with the great drone
Fera la rabardie.	he will play the dance.★
Cibalala du riaus du riaus,	*Chivalala . . .†*
Cibalala durie.	

★ *Rabardie*—dance with songs.

† Nonsense refrain.

Le Chansonnier de l'Arsenal, ed. P. Aubry (Paris, 1909), fol. 205.

2. Dist Guis: "ator
   Avrai meillor
   Ke j'encoires i voie;
   Tant de baudor
   Ferai, seignor,
   Ke l'onors en iert moie.
   Je voil mes cordouans cauchier
   Et s'avrai chapel de pronier

   Et ma cote faudée.
   Nus miex de la contrée
   De moi ne fet le rabardel;
   Bien sai noter au chalemel

   Et tote la maistrie."
   Cibalala . . .

Said Gui: "I shall be
more splendidly dressed
than ever before;
I shall provide
such amusement, sir,
that the honors will be mine.
I want to wear my leather shoes,
and I shall have my wreath of
   prune twigs
and my pleated tunic.
No one in the country
performs the rabardel better than I.
I know well how to play the cha-
   lumeau
and the whole art."
Chivalala . . .

3. Rogiers au tor
   Dist, par amor
   Donra Sarain coroie.
   Perrins color
   Mua, pavor
   A, tolir ne li doie.
   Lors li a dit en reprovier:
   "Rogier, bien l'i poes laissier,

   Sarre est bien assenée.
   Je croi k'iert espousée
   Entre chi et le quarremel.
   Guis i avra son taburel
   Et sa muse tesie."
   Cibalala . . .

Rogier in turn
said for love
he would give Sara a belt.
Perrin changed color,
is frightened;
he should not take her away.
Than he said to him reprovingly:
"Rogier, you had better leave it
   there.
Sara is too sensible.
I think she will be married
between now and Lent.
Gui will have his drum
and bagpipe filled [with money]."
Chivalala . . .

4. Au part destor
   Sans nul demor
   S'en vont et je m'avoie,

   En mon retor
   Truis au tabor
   Perrot deseur l'erboie,
   Ou fait danser et espringuier,

   Trepent baiselles et bovier;

   Mais Rogier point n'agrée,

   Bien set, Sarre est jurée
   Por qui empris ot le chembel.
   Guis dou tabor au flahutel

Without delay
they scattered
in all directions and I went on my
   way.
On my return
I found Perrot
with a drum on the grass,
where there was dancing and
   springing;
the girls and shepherds stamp their
   feet.
But Rogier does not at all ap-
   prove.
He knows well Sara is pledged
and by whom she has been caught.
Gui with drum and fife

Leur fait ceste estampie;
Cibalala . . .

plays for them this estampie;
Chivalala . . .

5. Rogier iror
   N'ot mais graignor
   Et dist: "je ne lairoie
   Por nule amor,
   Cest trahitor
   Perrin batre ne doie;
   Car il m'a trai en derrier,
   Mar se fist onques curratier."

Rogier was
never angrier
and said: "I shall not give up
for any love;
this traitor
Perrin should I not beat?
For he went behind my back.
For his misfortune he made himself a
   go-between."

Lors a mandé s'espée
Et teu gent assemblée
Ki ne sont mie kaurenel;
Perrin ont si oint le musel
K'il n'a talent k'il die:
Cibalala . . .

Then he asked for his sword
and assembled such people
as were not a bit cowardly.
They so anointed Perrin's muzzle
that he had no desire to sing:
Chivalala . . .

6. Quant je vi Perrin
      manier,
   Un petit me sui trais arrier,
   S'esgardai la mellée.
   Mainte coife tirée
   I ot et doné maint chembel.
   Guis s'i mist, de cop de cotel
   Fu sa muse perchie.
   Cibalala . . .

When I saw how Perrin was
      treated,
I drew back a little
and watched the melee.
Much hair was pulled
and many blows given.
Gui mixed in and a blow of a knife
pierced his bagpipe.
Chivalala . . .

46

GILLEBERT DE BERNEVILLE, *De moi dolereus*

Rotrouenge

De moi do - le - reus vos chant; Je fui nez en de - crois - sant.

N'on-ques n'euc en mon vi - vant Deus bons jors. *J'ai a nom: Mes-che-ans d'A-mors.*

1. De moi dolereus vos chant;
   Je fui nez en decroissant.

   N'onques n'euc en mon vivant
   Deus bons jors.
   J'ai a nom: Mescheans d'Amors.

2. Adés vois merci criant:
   "Amors, aidiés vo servant!"
   N'ainc n'i peuc trover noiant
   De secors.
   J'ai a nom: Mescheans d'Amors.

3. Hé, traitour mesdisant!
   Vos estes si mal parlant;
   Tolu avés maint amant
   Leur honors.
   J'ai a nom; Mescheans d'Amors.

4. Certes, piere d'aîmant
   Ne desirre le fer tant
   Com je sui d'un douz semblant
   Couvoitos.
   J'ai a nom: Mescheans d'Amors.

Of my sad self I sing to you.
I was born under a bad sign [the
   waning moon].
Never in my life have I had
two good days.
I am called Unlucky in Love.

Now I go crying for pity.
"Love, help your servant!"
Never do I find there
any succor.
I am called Unlucky in Love.

Hey, slandering traitor,
you speak such evil;
you have robbed many lovers
of their honor.
I am called Unlucky in Love.

Surely the magnet
does not desire iron as much
as I am covetous of
a sweet welcome.
I am called Unlucky in Love.

Beck M, p. 159v (fol. 174v).

47

Penser ne doit vilenie

Chanson with Refrains

I. 1. Pen - ser ne doit vi - le - ni - e 2. Cuers qui ai - me loi - au - ment,
3. Mais be - er a cor - toi - si - e 4. Et ha - ir vi - lai - ne gent;

II. 1. Gais, jo - lis to - te ma vi - e 2. Se - rai, et plus loi - au - ment
3. A - me - rai, que que nus di - e, 4. Ce - li ou mes cuers s'a - tent

III. 1. Do - né li ai sans bois - di - e 2. Mon fin cuer en - tie - re - ment;
3. Or doint Dex que o - tro - i - e 4. Me soit s'a - mor vrai - e - ment.

IV. 1. S'a - me - rai sanz tri - che - ri - e, 2. Si con - me j'oi et en - tent,
3. Cele ou il a cor - toi - si - e 4. Plus q'il n'en a en au - tre cent.

I. 5. Et a - mer plus hau - te - ment 6. Coin - te dame et en - voi - si - e.
II. 5. Por a - voir a - le - ge - ment 6. Des maus dont je quier a - i - e;
III. 5. A mains join - tes dou - ce - ment 6. Li proi que ne m'o-blit mi - e.
IV. 5. Tres - tout mes cuers a li - tent, 6. Bele est et bien en - sei - gni - e;

I. 7. S'a - me - rai la plus jo - li - e 8. Qu'en tres - tot le mon - de sai:
II. 7. Et s'il li plaist si m'o - ci - e, 8. Ja ne l'en sau - rai mau - gré:
III. 7. Tant est de biau - té gar - ni - e, 8. De sens ja n'en par - ti - rai:
IV. 7. Tant est belle et bien tai - lli - e, 8. Que je l'aim en bo - ne foi:

I. Ref. *J'ai, j'ai a - mo - re - tes Au cuer, qui me tie - nent gai.*

II. Ref. *A la plus sa - ve - rou - se - te Del mont ai mon cuer do - né.*

III. Ref. *A - - mo - re - tes ai, Jo - li - e - tes, s'a - me - rai.*

Beck M, p. 161v (fol. 176v).

IV. Ref. *Touz   li   cuer   me   rit   de   joi - e,   Quant   la   voi.*

Touz   li   cuer   me   rit   de   joi - e,   Quant   la   voi.

Touz   li   cuer   m'en   rit   de   joi - e,   quant   la   voi(e).

1. The heart that loves loyally should not consider an evil deed, but strive to be courteous and despise ignoble men; and love more deeply a gracious and pleasant lady. So shall I love the prettiest [one] I know in all the world. *I have, I have loves in my heart that keep me gay.*

2. Gay, agreeable I shall be all my life, and I shall love more faithfully, whatever anyone says, her from whom my heart expects to have relief from the pains for which I seek aid; and if it pleases her that I die, I shall feel no ill will. *To the most delightful [one] in the world I have given my heart.*

3. I have given her without deception my pure heart entirely; now may it please God that her love be granted me truly. With joined hands, gently I beg her not to forget me. Her beauty is so adorned with sense that I shall never leave her. *I have a love, pretty little love, so shall I love.*

4. So shall I love without treachery, as I hear and understand, her in whom there is more courtesy than in a hundred others. My heart always reaches toward her. She is beautiful and well brought up; so beautiful and well formed that I love her in good faith: *My whole heart laughs with joy when I see her.*

---

* The melody is missing in *Penser ne doit.* The three versions given here are taken from quotations in a motet, the *Cour de Paradis,* and the *Roman de Fauvel.*

48

NEIDHART VON REUENTHAL, *Ine gesach die heide*

Summer Song

1. Ine gesach die heide
   nie baz gestalt,
   in liehter ougenweide
   den grüenen walt:
   bî den beiden kiese wir den
     meien.
   Ir mägde, ir sult iuch zweien,

   gein dirre liehten sumerzît
   in hôhem muote reien.

2. Lop von mangen zungen
   der meie hât.
   Die bluomen sint entsprungen
   an manger stat,
   dâ man ê deheine kunde vin-
     den,
   geloubet stât diu linde:
   dâ hebt sich. als ich hân ver-
     nomen,
   ein tanz von höfschen kinden.

1. I never saw the heath
   in better shape,
   or a lovelier sight
   than the green wood;
   by both we recognize the May.

   You girls, you should find
     partners
   to welcome bright summer time
   in high-spirited dance.

2. May is praised
   by many tongues.
   Flowers have burst forth
   in many places
   where previously none could be
     found;
   the lime trees have put on leaves;
   a dance of courtly maidens is
     beginning,
   as I have learned.

DTÖ, p. 7 (fols. 153v–154).

3. Die sint sorgen âne
   und vröuden rîch.
   Ir mägede wolgetâne
   und minneclîch,
   zieret iuch, daz iu die Beier dan-
   ken,
   die Swâbe und die Vranken!

   Ir brîset iuwer hemde wîz
   mit sîden wol zen lanken!

They are free of worries
and full of joys.
You pretty
and love-worthy maidens,
bedeck yourselves so that the Ba-
varians,
Swabians and Franks may appreci-
ate you!
You trim your white shifts well
with silk to your hips.

4. "Gein wem solt ich mich
      zâfen?"
   sô redete ein maget.
   "Die tumben sint entslâfen;

   ich bin verzaget.
   Vreude und êre ist al der werlde
      unmaere.
   die man sint wandelbaere:
   deheiner wirbet umbe ein wîp,
   der er getiuwert waere."

"For whom should I primp myself?"
asks one of the maidens.
"The stupid men have fallen
   asleep;
I am in despair.
Joy and honour are of no account
   to the world.
Men are inconstant:
none woos a woman
to whom he would be true.

5. "Die rede soltû behalten,"
   sprach ir gespil.
   "Mit vröuden sul wir alten:

   der manne ist vil,
   die noch gerne dienent guoten
      wîben.
   Lât solhe rede belîben!
   Ez wirbet einer umbe mich,
   der trûren kan vertrîben."

"Don't talk rubbish,"
said her companion.
"Old age should come through
   joys:
There are still lots of men
who still serve good women
   gladly.
Cease such chatter!
Wooing me is one
who can chase away sorrow."

6. "Den soltû mir zeigen,
   wier mir behage.
   Der gürtel sî dîn eigen,
   den umbe ich trage!
   Sage mir sînen namen, der dich
      minne
   sô tougenlicher sinne!
   Mir ist getroumet hînt von dir,
   dîn muot der stê von hinne."

"You must show him to me,
how he would appeal to me.
Let the girdle
I am wearing be yours!
Tell me his name, who woos you

in such secret manner.
I dreamt last night
that you have a mind to be gone
   from here."

7. "Den si alle nennent
   von Riuwental,
   und sînen sanc erkennent

"The one they all call
Reuental,
and whose songs are known

wol über al,
derst mir holt. Mit guote ich
  im des lône:
durch sînen willen schône

so wil ich brîsen mînen lip.
Wol dan, man liutet nône!"

everywhere above all others,
he is partial to me. With goodness
  I reward him for that:
because of his excellent suggestions,
I'll adorn my body.
Well then, they're ringing nones!"

49

NEIDHART VON REUENTHAL, *Owê, lieber sumer*

Winter Song

O - wê, lie - ber su - mer, dî - ne lieh - ten ta - ge lan - ge,
Gar ge - swei - get sint diu vo - ge - lîn mit ir ge - san - ge;

Wie die sint ver - kê - ret an ir schî - ne!
Doch ist daz diu mei - ste sor - ge mî - ne,

Si truo - bent un - de ne - ment an ir süe - zem we - ter a - be.
Daz mir niht lang - er die - nest lie - ben lôn er - wor - ben ha - be.

Ich en - kund' ir lei - der nie ge - spre - chen noch ge - sin - gen,

Daz die wol - ge - tâ - nen diuh - te lô - nes wert.

Lô - nâ, kü - ne - ginn'! ich bin, der lô - nes gert:

Lie - bist al - ler wîb, ich hân ûf lie - ben lôn ge - din - gen.

1. Owê, lieber sumer, dîne liehten tage lange, Wie die sint verkêret an ir schîne! Si truobent unde nement an ir süezem weter abe.	Ah, dear summer, your clear long days, how they have lost their brightness. They became cloudy and the gentle weather is gone.

DTÖ, p. 17 (fols. 238–238v).

Gar gesweiget sint diu vogelîn
    mit ir gesange;
Doch ist daz diu meiste sorge
    mîne,
Daz mir niht langer dienest
    lieben lôn erworben habe.
Ich enkunde ir leider nie ge-
    sprechen noch gesingen,
Daz die wolgetänen diuhte
    lönes wert.
Lônâ, küneginne! ich bin, der
    lônes gert:
Liebist aller wîbe, ich han ûf
    lieben lôn gedingen.

Utterly stilled are the little birds
    with their song.
But what gives me most grief

is that long service has not won
    me a sweet reward.
I could not, alas, say or sing to her

anything she thought worth re-
    warding.
Reward me, my queen! I ask for
    my reward.
Dearest of all women, I have
    earned a sweet reward.

2. Hât ab iemen leit, daz mînem
    leide sich gelîche,
Möhte mir der sînen rât en-
    bieten!
Deiswâr, guoter raete der be-
    dörfte niemen baz.
Ich gespraeche mîne vriunde
    gerne sumelîche,
Daz si mir von solhen sorgen
    rieten:
Mich vêhet âne schulde, der ich
    selten ie vergaz.

Daz ist wunder, daz ich eine
    wîle vrô belîbe,
Sît daz mich diu guote in un-
    genâden hât.
Wan daz mich mîn triuwe und
    ouch mîn staete enlât.
Ich geslüege nimmer niuwez
    liet deheinem wîbe.

If someone had a sorrow like
    mine,
may he offer me his advice!

It's true, no one is more in need of
    good advice.
I freely talked it over with my
    friends,
so that they might give me guid-
    ance about such worries.
I met with such undeserved hos-
    tility that I have not forgotten
    it.
It's remarkable that I have re-
    mained content,
since I am out of favor with my
    good lady.
If it weren't for my fidelity and
    constancy,
I would never sing a new song for
    a woman.

3. Ine gewan vor mangen zîten
    ungenâde mêre,
Danne ich hân von einem
    getelinge:
Derst alsô getoufet, daz in
    niemen nennen sol.
Der ist an sîner strâze beidiu
    tretzic unde hêre.
Langez swert alsam ein hanif-
    swinge,

I have never received as much an-
    noyance
as from a certain village oaf.

He is christened, so no one should
    name him.
In his street he is aggressive and
    superior;
with a sword as long as a hemp
    swingle

Daz treit er allez umbe; im ist
    sîn gehilze hol.
Dâ sint luoger in gemachet,
    zeine zîzelwaehe;
Oben in dem knophe lît ein
    spiegelglas,
Dem gelîch alsô daz Friderûnen
    was.
Dô bat er die guoten, daz si
    sich dar inne ersaehe.

4. Sîne wolde iedoch in sînen
    spiegel nie geluogen:
Daz versagtes im in einer
    smaehe;
Si sprach verwendeclîchen:
    "Daz ist immer ungetân.

Ich bekenne iuch niht an iuwer
    hôvescheit sô kluogen.

Ê ez iu ze liebe an mir ge-
    schaehe,
Jâ wolde ich ê verliesen slehtes
    allez, daz ich hân."
Sî sprach: "Liupper, heime ich
    hân noch guoter spiegel drîe:
Derst mir iegelîcher lieber
    danne der."
Schiere sprach er aber: "Vrou-
    we, luoget her!"
Alsô müete sî der gouch mit
    sîner hoppenîe.

5. Hie mit disen dingen sî diu rede
    alsô gescheiden!
Lât iu mêre künden mîner
    swaere!
Die tumben getelinge tuont
    mir aller leideclîch.
Swaz ich tuon, ich kan si bî der
    guoten niht erleiden.
Wessen sî, wie lîhte ich des en-
    baere,

Si würben anderthalben, Gîsel-
    breht und Amelrîch:

he smashes everything; his scab-
    bard is empty.
There are holes made in it, and
    braided tassles;
in the hilt there is a mirror

similar to Friderun's.

He asked the lady to look at her-
    self in it.

She, however, did not want to
    look at herself in his mirror.
Disdainfully she denied him that.

Turning her head away, she
    spoke: "That is always un-
    couth.
You have put on such clever,
    courtly airs that I don't recog-
    nize you.
Before I am forced to please you,

I would rather lose everything I
    have."
She said, "My dear fellow, I have
    three good mirrors at home.
I prefer any one of them to that
    one."
But immediately he said: "Lady,
    look here!"
Thus the oaf bothered her with
    his importunity.

May the speech have ended with
    these things.
Let me tell you more of my prob-
    lems.
The dumb yokels all affront me.

Whatever I do, I can't stand them
    around my lady.
If Giselbrecht and Amelrich knew
    how easily I could do without
    them
if they wooed elsewhere.

Die hânt disen sumer her
  getanzet an ir hende
Allenthalben, swâ man ie der
  vreuden phlac.
Hinne vür gelebe ich nimmer
  lieben tac,
Unze ich mînen kumber nâch
  dem willen mîn volende.

All summer they have danced at-
  tendance on her
everywhere when one was having
  fun.
From now on I shall never enjoy a
  pleasant day
until I finish describing my sorrow to my satisfaction.

50

Laude novella sia cantata

Italian Lauda

Laude novella sia cantata	*Let a new song of praise be sung*
A l'alta donna encoronata.	*to the noble crowned lady.*
1. Fresca vergene donçella,	Fresh virgin maid,
Primo fior, rosa novella,	first flower, new rose,
Tutto'l mondo a te s'apella;	the whole world appeals to thee,
Nella bonor fosti nata.†	thou wert born in happiness.
Laude novella . . .	*Let a new song . . .*

---

* The notes of the last phrase are a third lower in the manuscript than those given here, an obvious scribal error.

† The return of the refrain rhyme in the last line of each stanza clearly points to the repetitions of the refrain indicated here.

Facsimile in F. Liuzzi, *La Lauda e i primordi della melodia italiana* (Rome, 1935), Vol. I, facing p. 261.

2. Fonte se' d'aqqua surgente

Madre de Dio vivente;
Tu se' luce de la gente,
Sovra li angeli exalta.
Laude novella . . .

Thou art a fountain of spring
water,
mother of the living God;
thou art the light of the people,
exalted above the angels.
Let a new song . . .

3. Tu se' verga, tu se' fiore,

Tu se' luna de splendore;
Voluntà avemo e core
De venir a te, ornata.
Laude novella . . .

Thou art the branch, thou art the
flower,
thou art the moon of splendor;
we have the will and the heart
to come to thee, adorned one.
Let a new song . . .

4. Tu se' rosa, tu se' gillio,
Tu portasti el dolce fillio;
Però, donna, sì m'enpillio
De laudar te, honorata.
Laude novella . . .

Thou art the rose, thou art the lily,
thou borest the sweet son;
therefore, I thus set to work
to praise thee, distinguished lady.
Let a new song . . .

5. Archa se' d'umulitade,
Vaso d'ogne sanctitade;
En te venne deitade;
D'angel foste salutata.
Laude novella . . .

Thou art the ark of humility,
vessel of all sanctity;
in thee came the deity;
thou wert saluted by the angel.
Let a new song . . .

6. De le vergin' se' verdore,
De le spose se' honore;
A tutt(a) gente port' amore,
Tanto se' ingratiata.
Laude novella . . .

Of virgins thou art the verdure,
of wives thou art the honor;
to all people thou bringest love,
so much art thou full of grace.
Let a new song . . .

7. Nulla lingua pò contare
Come tu se' da laudare;
Lo tuo nome fa tremare
Sathanas a mille fiata.
Laude novella . . .

No tongue can tell
how thou art to be praised;
thy name makes Satan
tremble a thousand times.
Let a new song . . .

8. Pregot', avocata mia
Ke ne metti en bona via;
Questa nostra compania
Siate sempre commendata.
Laude novella . . .

I pray thee, my advocate, —
to put us on the good way;
may this our company
always be commended to thee.
Let a new song . . .

9. Commendan te questa terra
Che la guardi d'ogne guerra;
Ben s'enganna e trop' erra

Ki t'afende, O Beata.
Laude novella . . .

They commend to thee this land,
that thou keepest it from all war;
he much deceives himself and too
much errs
who vexes thee, O Blessed.
Let a new song . . .

51

Santa Maria amar

Cantiga de Santa Maria (No. 7)

Esta e como Santa Maria
  livrou a abadessa prenne,
que adormecera ant' o seu altar
  chorando.

Santa Maria amar
Devemos muit' e rogar
Qua a ssa graça ponna
Sobre nos, porque errar
Non nos faça, nen peccar,
O demo sen vergonna.

I. Porende vos contarey
  D'un miragre que achei

This is how Holy Mary protected
  a pregnant abbess
who fell asleep weeping before her
  altar.

We should love Holy Mary
very much and beseech
that with Her grace
She cover us, so that
the devil without shame
may not make us go astray or sin.

Therefore I shall tell you
  of a miracle that took place,

H. Anglès, *La Musica de las Cantigas de Santa Maria* **(Barcelona, 1964), Vol. I, fols. 36v–37.**

Que por hũa badessa
Fez a Madre do gran Rei,
Ca, per com' eu apres' ei,
Eraxe sua essa.
Mas o demo enartar
A foi, porque emprennar
S'ouve d'un de Bolonna,
Ome que de recadar
Avia, e de guardar,
Seu feit'e sa besonna.
Santa Maria amar . . .

which the Mother of God
performed for an abbess,
because, as I have since learned,
she herself was there.
But the devil deceived her
so that she became pregnant
by one from Bologna,
a man who should have received
and kept secret
her act and her misdeed.
We should love Holy Mary . . .

II. As monjas, pois entender

Foron esto e saber,
Ouveron gran lediça;
Ca, porque lles non sofrer
Queria de mal fazer,
Avian-lle mayça.
E fórona acusar,
Ao Bispo do logar,
E el ben de Collonna
Chegou y; e pois chamar
A fez, vẽo sen vagar,
Leda e mui risonna.
Santa Maria amar . . .

The nuns, when they had per-
ceived
and became certain of this,
were greatly pleased,
for, because she would
permit them no mischief,
they held some malice toward her.
And they made accusations
to the bishop of the place,
and he came there from Cologne.
And when he summoned her,
she came without delay,
joyous and very cheerful.
We should love Holy Mary . . .

III. O Bispo lles diss' assi:
"Dona, per quant' aprendi,
Mui mal vossa fazenda
Fezestes; e vin aqui
Por esto, que ante mi
Façades end' emenda."
Mas a dona sen tardar
A Madre de Deus rogar

The bishop spoke to her thus:
"Lady, from what I have heard,
you have behaved very badly;
and I have come here
so that before me
you may repent and reform."
But the lady, without waiting,
went to beseech the Mother of
God;

Foi; e, come quen sonna,
Santa Maria tirar
Lle fez o fill' e criar
Lo mandou en Sanssonna.
Santa Maria amar . . .

and as she slept, Holy Mary
delivered her
of the child and sent it
to be raised in Soissons.*
We should love Holy Mary . . .

IV. Pois s' a dona espertou
E se guarida achou,
Log' ant' o Bispo vẽo;

When the lady awoke
and found herself cured,
she presently came before the
bishop;

---

* The rhymes of the refrain, which are repeated in the second half of each stanza, probably dictated the poet's choice of Cologne, Bologna (or Boulogne?), and Soissons as
place names.

E el muito a catou
E desnua-la mandou;
E pois lle vyu o sẽo,
Começou Deus a loar
E as donas a brasmar,
Que eran d'ordin d'Onna,
Dizendo: "Se Deus m'anpar,
Por salva poss' esta dar,
Que non sei que ll'aponna."

Santa Maria amar . . .

and he examined her closely
and ordered her to be stripped.
And when he saw her
he began to praise God
and to censure the nuns,
who were of the order of Onna,*
saying: "If God be my help,
I can declare her innocent,
for I do not know of what she may
    be accused."

We should love Holy Mary . . .

---

* *Onna:* Oña, a municipality in the province of Burgos. A sly joke may be intended here. Legend had it that the monastery of San Salvator de Oña, originally peopled by both men and women, was founded by the son of a Countess Onna to make amends for her execution because of her depraved love for a Musulman. Indeed, Alfonso the Wise himself recorded this erroneous tale.

52

Byrd one brere

English Love Song

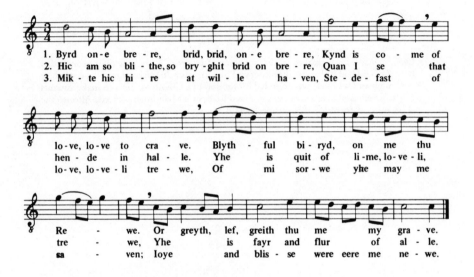

1. Byrd on-e bre-re, brid, brid, on-e bre-re, Kynd is co-me of lo-ve, lo-ve to cra-ve. Blyth-ful bi-ryd, on me thu Re-we. Or greyth, lef, greith thu me my gra-ve.

2. Hic am so bli-the, so bry-ght brid on bre-re, Quan I se that hen-de in hal-le. Yhe is quit of li-me, lo-ve-li, tre-we, Yhe is fayr and flur of al-le.

3. Mik-te hic hi-re at wil-le ha-ven, Ste-de-fast of lo-ve, lo-ve-li tre-we, Of mi sor-we yhe may me sa-ven; Ioye and blis-se were eere me ne-we.

1. Bird on a briar, bird, bird on a briar,
   Mankind is come of love, love to crave.
   Blitheful bird, on me have mercy
   or build, love, build thou me my grave.

2. I am as blithe as a bright bird on a briar
   When I see that maid in the hall.
   She is white of limb, lovely, true,
   She is fair and flower of all.

3. Might I have her at will,
   Steadfast of love, lovely, true,
   Of my sorrow she might save me,
   Joy and bliss were ever to me new.

Facsimile in J. Saltmarsh, "Two Medieval Love-Songs set to Music," *Antiquaries Journal,* XV (1935), facing p. 3. The transcription follows the apparent note values of the original, with no attempt to force them into regular measures of triple meter.

53

Dame de valur—Hei Diex! cant je
remir—Amoris

Motet Enté

1) Amoris

2)

Tu, fol. 6v (*Mo*, fol. 320, *Ba*, fol. 22).

Triplum:
Lady of worth and goodness, full of love and of great beauty, by you I am so taken and so caught that all my thoughsts are of you. From my heart without falseness I shall thus sing of her: *"I have a pretty little love, so shall I love!"*
Ah, God! most gentle God! Oh! I know well that I shall die of it! But her great goodness keeps my heart alive sweetly, for I have served her loyally.

Duplum:
Ah, God! when I regard her joyous person! Ah, God! I shall love her even more, for no one more pleasing have I known in my life! But when I see her eyes glancing, her mouth laughing, God! I never saw anyone so beautiful! Ah, God! the most sweet God! I shall love her still, for no other than she pleases me so much.

54

Aucun vont—Amor qui cor—Kyrie

Bilingual Motet

Au-cun vont so-vent Por lor en-vi-e Mes-di-sant d'a-mur, Mais ilh n'est si bo-ne vi-e Com

A - mor___ qui cor___ vul - ne -

1) Kyrie eleison*

d'a-mer loi - au - ment; Car d'a-meir vient to-te cor-toi-si - e,

rat Hu - ma - num, quem ge - ne -

Tote ho-nur Et tos biens en-sen - gne - mens. Tot ce puet en li

rat Car - na - lis af - fe - cti - o,

Tu, fol. 13 (*Mo*, fol. 290v). Kyrie: *LU*, p. 40.

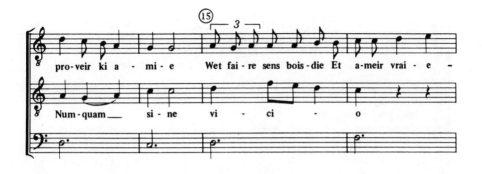

pro-veir ki a - mi - e   Wet fai - re sens bois-die Et a-meir vrai - e -

Num-quam___ si - ne vi - ci - o

ment,   Car ja en li n'iert as - si - se Vi-lo-ni - e   Ne con-voi - ti -

Vel ra - ro pot - est es - se,

se D'a-mas-seir ar - gent,   Ains ai-me bu-ne com-pa-gnie Et des-

Quo - ni - am est ne - ces - se

2)

pent a-des lar - ge-ment,Et si n'at en li fe - lo - ni - e N'en-vi - e Sor au-tre

Ex quo___ plus di - li - gi - tur

Triplum:

Some, through envy, often speak ill of love; but there is no life so good as
loving loyally. For from loving comes all courtesy, all honor, and all good
breeding. All this can one experience who wishes without falseness to have
a lover and to love truly; for never in him will there be villainy or cove-
tousness to amass money. But he loves good company and spends freely;
and in him is no treachery nor envy of others. But he is humble to all and
speaks courteously, if he has wholly, without division, given his heart entirely to loving. And you may know that he loves not at all, but lies, if he
conducts himself otherwise.

Duplum:

Love that wounds the human heart, that carnal affection generates, can
never, or rarely, be without vice, since necessarily, the more a thing that
quickly escapes or passes is loved, the less the Lord is loved.

55

C'est la jus—Pro patribus

Motet with Rondeau Text

It's down there in the meadow
She gave me her love.
The little spring there runs clear.
False peasants, withdraw from there;
She gave me her love
Who has my heart and my body.

Paris, Bibl. nat., fr. 12615, fol. 195.

56

J'ai les maus d'amours—Que ferai—In seculum

Rondeau-Motet Enté

Triplum:
I have the pains of love without suffering when *she gave me her love who has my heart and my love.* And since she has it, I well know that she will kill me.

Duplum:
What shall I do, good Lord God? *The glance of her green eyes* I shall await to have better grace. *The glance of her green eyes kills me.*

57

Dansse Real

Instrumental Dance

58

Trotto

Instrumental Dance

Prima pars.
2
Secunda pars.
Terza pars.
Quarta pars.
Quinta pars.

* Cues for returning to the *prima pars* are as given in the manuscript.

London, Brit. Mus., add., 29987, fol. 62v. Facsimile of the manuscript in Musicological Studies and Documents 13 (American Institute of Musicology, 1965).

59

PHILIPPE DE VITRY, *Garrit Gallus—In nova fert—Neuma*

Isorhythmic Motet

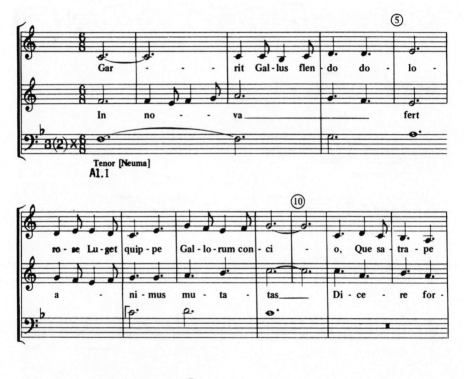

Pic (Fauv, fol. 44v). Facsimile in NPM, p. 331.

se - dens of - fi - ci - o. At - que vul - pes, tam -

ne - quam quam o - lim pe - ni - tus mi - ra -

quam vi - spi - li - o in Be - li - al vi - gens a - stu - ci - a

- bi - lis cru - cis po - ten - ci - a

II

De_____ le - o - nis con - sen - su pro - pri - o

De - bel - la - vit Mi - cha - el in - cli - tus,___

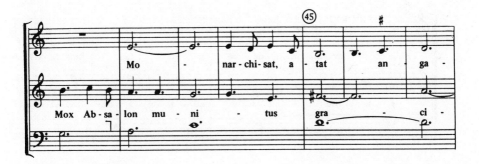

Mo - nar - chi - sat, a - tat an - ga -

Mox Ab - sa - lon mu - ni - tus gra - ci -

ri - a. Rur - sus, ec - ce, Ja - cob fa - mi - li - a Pha - ra - o - ne al-

- - a, Mox U - li - xis gau - dens fa - cun - di -

III

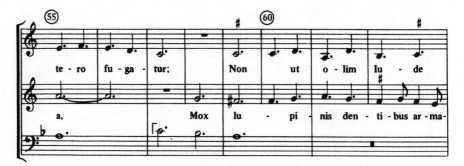

te - ro fu - ga - tur; Non ut o - lim Iu - de -

a, Mox lu - pi - nis den - ti - bus ar - ma -

ve - sti - gi - a Sub - in - tra - re po - tens,

tus, _____ Sub Ter - - - -

la - cri - ma - tur. In de - ser - to fa - me fla - gel - la -

si - tis mi - les mi - li - ci - a Rur - sus vi - vit in

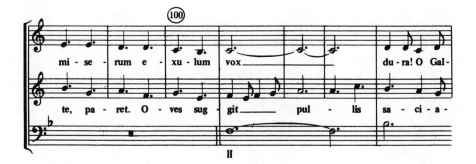

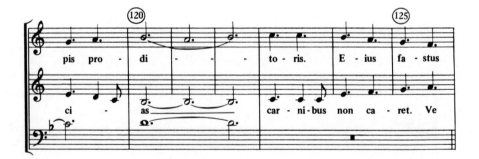

III

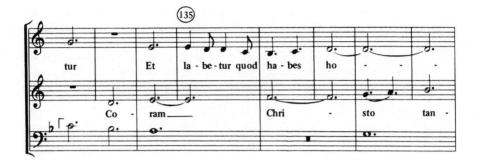

Triplum:

The cock babbles, lamenting sorrowfully, for the whole assembly of cocks* mourns because, while serving vigilantly, it is trickily betrayed by the satrap. And the fox,† like a grave robber, thriving with the astuteness of Belial, rules as monarch with the consent of the lion himself.‡ Ah, what slavery! Lo, once again Jacob's family is exiled by another Pharaoh. Not, as formerly, able to escape to the homeland of Judah, they weep. Stricken by hunger in the desert, lacking the help of arms, although they cry out, they are robbed; perhaps speedily they will die. O harsh voice of the wretched exiles! O sorrowful babbling of the cocks, since the dark blindness of the lion submits to the fraud of the traitorous fox. You who suffer the arrogance of his misdeeds, rise up, or what you have of honor is being or will be lost, because if avengers are slow men soon turn to evil doing.

Duplum:

My heart is set upon speaking of forms changed into new (bodies).§ The evil dragon that renowned Michael once utterly defeated by the miraculous power of the Cross, now endowed with the grace of Absalom, now with

---

* *Gallus:* cock; or Gauls (the French).

† Enguerran de Marigny, chief councillor of the French king.

‡ Philip IV the Fair.

§ Ovid, *Metamorphoses,* 1, 1.

the cheerful eloquence of Ulysses, now armed with wolfish teeth a soldier in the service of Thersites, lives again changed into a fox whose tail the lion deprived of sight obeys, while the fox reigns. He sucks the blood of sheep and is satiated with chickens. Alas, he does not cease sucking and still thirsts; he does not abstain from meats at the wedding feast. Woe now to the chickens, woe to the blind lion. In the presence of Christ, finally, woe to the dragon.

60

Se je chant

Chace

Se je chant mains que____ ne____ suel____

Se je chant mains que____ ne____ suel____

De la sim - ple sans or - guel Ou j'ai mis tou-te ma____

Se je chant mains que____ ne____ suel____

De la__ sim - ple sans or - guel Ou j'ai mis tou-te ma____

cu - re En i - ver pour la froi - du - - re,

Pic, facsimile in *MGG* I, cols. 715/16 (Ivrea, Bibl. Capitolare, [without signature], fol. 52v).

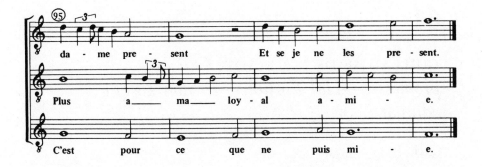

If I sing less than usual of the simple modest one to whom I am wholly devoted in the cold of winter, it is for love of the falcons that I have, so fine and so good at hunting by the river that I hold nothing so dear as to go there often when the air is clear and not too windy. Let's go, gentle comrades, the birds are down there.

Ho—don't speak! Ho—I see them! Ho—cast off, cast off or you lose them. Huo, huo, houp . . . He's getting away. Hau, ha hau, ho hau, houp! He's onto the trick, God willing. Hou, ha hau . . . pick him up! Hau ha hau—he's dead. Let's feed our falcons now. Hau hau ha ha hau.

Good gentle comrades, let us return, since we find no more birds to hunt in this countryside. Of those we have taken here I shall make my lady a present. And if I no longer give them to my loyal friend, it is because I can't.

61

GUILLAUME DE MACHAUT, *Qui es promesses—Ha! Fortune—Et non est qui adjuvat*

Isorhythmic Motet

Mach A, fol. 421v.

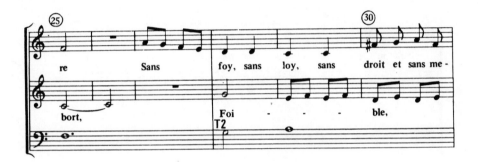

pan. iso in all parts

de faus- se fi - gu - re; Et li siens sont tou - dis en

sort, Ne riens de bien pour moy, car

a - ven - tu - re De tre - bu - chier, car, par droi - te na - tu -

sans rai - son Je voy ve-nir la mort a - mere a
C3

re, La des - loy - al re - no - y - e, par-

tort Pre - ste
T4

ju - re, Faus - se, trai - tre, per - verse et me - re su - re

de moy mettre a

Triplum:

Who trusts in the promises of Fortune and feels secure in the riches of her gifts, or he who believes her to be so much his friend that for him she will be firm or sure in anything, he is too foolish, for she is not sure, without faith, without law, without justice and without measure, it's excrement covered with rich covering, which gleams without and within is ordure. She is an idol of false portraiture in whom none should believe nor trust for protection; her virtuous propriety does not last, for it is all wind, nor can anything she represents be other than a false figure; and her followers are always in danger of falling, for, by her true nature, disloyal Fortune denies, perjures; false, traitorous, perverse and sour mother, she soothes and then pierces with such mortal wounds that those whom she has nourished she traitorously destroys.

Duplum:

Ha, Fortune, I am placed too far from port when you put me on the sea without an oar in a little boat, flat and without sides, weak, rotten, without a sail; and about (me) all the winds are contrary to bring about my death, so that there is no comfort nor salvation, pity, nor hope, nor means of escape, nor anything good for me; for without reason I see bitter death coming unjustly, ready to destroy me; but this death I receive through your spell, false Fortune, and through your treachery.

Tenor:

And there is no one who helps.

62

MACHAUT, *Dous amis*

Ballade

Dous a - mis, oy mon com - plaint: A toy
Mes cuers qu'a - mours si con - traint Que tiens

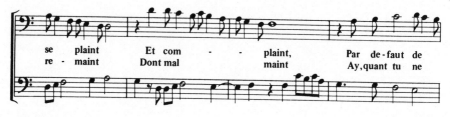

se plaint Et com - plaint, Par de - faut de
re - maint Dont mal maint Ay, quant tu ne

tes se - - cours,
me se - cours.

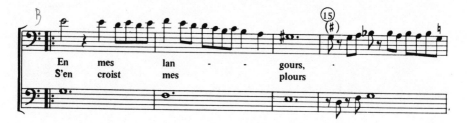

En mes lan - gours,
S'en croist mes plours

Mach A, fol. 456v. Facsimile in *NPM*, p. 357.

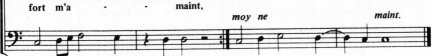

1. Dous amis, oy mon complaint:
   A toy se plaint
   Et complaint,
   Par defaut de tes secours,
   Mes cuers qu'amours si con-
   traint
   Que tiens remaint
   Dont mal maint
   Ay, quant tu ne me secours
   En mes langours,
   Car d'aillours
   N'est riens qui confort
   m'amaint.
   S'en croist mes plours
   Tous les jours,
   Quant tes cuers en moy ne maint.

   Gentle friend, hear my complaint:
   To you laments
   and complains,
   for want of your succour,
   my whole self, whom love so
   constrains
   that I am held fast,
   from which I have great pain,
   when you do not succour me
   in my weakness;
   for otherwise
   there is nothing that brings me
   comfort.
   Thus my tears increase
   every day,
   *when your whole self does not dwell
   in me.*

2. Amis, t'amour si m'ataint
   Que mon vis taint
   Et destaint
   Souvent de pluseurs coulours,
   Et mon dolent cuer estraint;
   Si le destraint
   Qu'il estaint
   Quant en toy n'a son recours.

   S'a jours trop cours
   Se n'acours
   Pour li garir, car il creint
   Mort, qui d'amours

   Friend, your love so attacks me
   that my face flushes
   and pales
   often with several colors,
   and grips my sorrowing heart;
   so constricts it
   that it ceases to beat
   when it does not find refuge in
   you.
   So its days are too short
   if you do not hasten
   to cure it, for it fears
   death, which results

Vient le cours,
Quant tes cuers en moy ne maint.

from love,
when your whole self does not dwell in me.

3. Mon cuer t'amour si ensaint
Qu'il ne se faint
Qu'il ne t'aint
Pour tes parfaites doucours;
Et ta biaute qui tout vaint

Dedens li paint
Et empraint
Avec tes hautes valours.
S'en sont gringnours
Mes dolours
Et plus dolereus mi plaint
Et en decours
Mes vigours,
Quant tes cuers en moy ne maint.

Your love so wounds my heart
that it does not pretend
that it does not love you
for your perfect charms;
and your beauty, which conquers all,

penetrates within it
and imprints (it)
with your great virtues.
So from this are my sorrows great
and more dolorous my plaint
and my strength
in decline,
when your whole self does not dwell in me.

63

MACHAUT, *Se vous n'estes*

Rondeau

Mach A, fol. 477v. Contratenor: *Mach E*, fol. 134. Alternate Contratenor: *Mod*, fol. 6v.

* The Contratenor in *Mod* appears to have three different endings, which are written
  successively as numbered in the score. Perhaps they are to be used in this order for
  the three statements of the rondeau's second section (2, 6, and 8).

If you are not born to be my reward,
Lady, in an ill hour I saw your soft laughing look.
Never will joy be awarded me,
If you are not born to be my reward,
For by you will grievous war be given me
That will make me die in battle.
If you are not born to be my reward,
Lady, in an ill hour I saw your soft laughing look.

64

MACHAUT, *De bonté, de valour*

Virelai

Refrain

1.5. De bon - té, de va - lour, De biau - té,
De ma - nie - re, d'a - tour, De sens, de
4. Jue - net - te, sans fo - lour, Sim - plet - te,
Par - faite en toute hon - nour, Nul - le n'est

de dou - cour Ma - dame est pa - ré - e;
grace est cou - ron - né - e.
sans bau - dour, De bonne heu - re né - e,
a vous com - pa - ré - e.

b verses
2. Da - me de - si - ré - e, Ri - che - ment a - our -
3. Bien en doc - tri - né - e, De tous a droit lo -

né - e De co - lour,
-é - e, Par sa - vour,

I.	1. De bonté, de valour,	With goodness, courage,
	De biauté, de doucour	beauty, and gentleness
	Ma dame est parée;	my lady is adorned;
	De maniere, d'atour,	with manners, dress,
	De sens, de grace est	sense and grace is she crowned.
	couronée.	
	2. Dame desirée,	Desired lady,
	Richement aournée	richly adorned
	De colour,	with color,
	3. Bien endoctrinée	well instructed,
	De tous a droit loée,	by all rightly praised
	Par savour,	for taste,

Mach A, fol. 484v.

	4. Juenette, sans folour,
	Simplette, sans baudour,
	De bonne heure née,
	Parfaite en toute hon-
	    nour,
	Nulle n'est a vous com-
	    parée.
		youthful without folly,
		simple without boldness,
		born in a happy hour,
		perfect in all honor,
		
		none can be compared to you.

	5. *De bonté, de valour . . .*	*With goodness, courage . . .*
II.	6. Car loyal, sacrée, De bonne renommée, Sans faus tour,	For loyal, dedicated, of good renown, without false tricks,
	7. Franche et esmerée, Nette, pure, affinée, La millour	frank and gracious, without stain, pure, refined, the best

	8. De toutes et la flour
	Sans mal, sans deshon-
	    nour,
	Estes apellée.
	Pour ce avez sans retour
	Mon cuer, m'amour et
	    ma pensée.
		of all and the flower
		without evil, without dishonor,
		
		you are called.
		For this you have eternally
		my heart, my love, and my mind.

	9. *De bonté, de valour . . .*	*With goodness, courage . . .*
III.	10. Et s'il vous agrée, Gentil dame honnourée, Que j'aour,	And if it pleases you, gentle, honored lady, that I adore,
	11. Qu'en moy soit doub- lée, Sans estre ja finée, Ma langour,	May in me be doubled, without ever coming to an end, my pining;

	12. Si vueil je la dolour
	Et l'amoureuse ardour
	Qu'en moy est entrée,
	Endurer nuit et jour,
	Ne ja n'en serez meins
	    amée.
		So I wish the pain
		and the amorous ardor
		that has entered within me
		to endure night and day,
		nor will you ever be loved less for
		    that.

	13. *De bonté, de valour . . .*	*With goodness, courage . . .*

65

LORENZO DA FIRENZE, *Dà, dà a chi avareggia*

Madrigal

1. Give, give, even to him who hoards for himself, If (bad) times
   come his way at the whim of a she-bear, Because without a purse
   one does not find a friend.
2. You, O you who have a (good) position, listen to me: He has a
   chance to make a friend for himself Who has his foot in the water,
   his beak in the millet.
Rit. Think now, think that he who falls, slowly refits the arrow to the
   bow to rise again (slowly helps himself to rise again). Woe to him
   whose turn it is.

66

NICCOLÒ DA PERUGIA, *Dappoi che'l sole*

Caccia

FL, fol. 82v. Also in published facsimile of London, Brit. Mus., add. 29987 (fol. 40v) (see No. 58, p. 119).

To-sto to - sto, che'l fuo-co pur s'a-pi - glia."

"Al-larm', al-lar - me!" "Tu to' la cier - vel - li - ra, La scu -

"Man-da per lla fa-mi - glia!" "Al-l'ac-qu'al-l'ac - qua! Su con le me -

r'e lla gor-gie - ra, To-sto to - sto, che'l

zi - - - - - - - ne!"

fuo-co pur s'a-pi - glia." "Man-da per lla fa - mi - glia!" "Al-l'ac-qu'al-l'ac - qua!

Chi por - ta doc - ce, chi re - ca - va sca - le,

Su con le me - zi - - - - - - ne!"

chi ru – ba – – va   E qual ac–qua ver–

dri – – – – to!"   Chi

sa – – va   E tal rom–pe – a   l'u–

sgon–bra e   chi ru – ba – – va   E qual

scio   con l'ac–cet – – ta.

ac–qua ver–sa – – va   E tal rom–pe

Qui o–gnun's'af–fret – ta   Pur d'a–mor za–re'l

a   l'u–scio con l'ac–cet – – ta.

After the sun hides its gentle rays and the moon reveals its splendor, I heard a great uproar, loud cries: "Fire, fire!" And then, waiting a bit: "Where is it, where is it?"—"It's here. Up up, everyone up. Get out the lamps, torches with lanterns. O you of the bell, ring! Don don don don. Alarm, alarm! You, grab the helmet, the axe, the gorget. Quick, quick, lest the fire really take hold. Send for the family. Water, water! Up with the jugs!" Some carry sprinklers, some fetched ladders, some hurt themselves, and some said: "Run here, oh help!" "Oh you of the trumpet, blow! Tatin, tatin. Everyone move to the right!" Some clear out, and some stole, and some poured water, and some broke the door with a hatchet. Then everyone hurries to put out the fire and the sparks. Passed were the noises, when the masters with great authority cried: "Everyone go home. It's out." Returning, I saw and always have in my heart, Ci ci with li and a (Cicilia).

67

FRANCESCO LANDINI, *Questa fanciull' amor*

Ballata

I. 1. **(A)** *Questa fanciull' amor fal-*
         lami pia
         Che m'a ferito'l cor nella
         tuo via.

   2. **(b)** Tu m'a, fanciulla, si
            d'amor percosso,
            Che solo in te pensando
            trovo posa.

   3. **(b)** El cor di me da me tu ai
            rimoso

This girl, love, make her kindly
toward me,
for she has wounded my heart in your
way.

You, girl, have so stricken my
heart with love
that only in thinking of you do I
find repose.

My heart from me you have re-
moved

Cogli ochi belli et la faccia gioiosa.

with your beautiful eyes and joyous face.

4. **(a)** Però al servo tuo de! sie pietosa
Mercè ti chiegho alla gram pena mia.

Yet to your servant, alas, be compassionate!
Mercy I beg of you for my great suffering.

5. **(A)** *Questa fanciull' amor . . .*

This girl, Love. . .

II. 6. **(b)** Se non soccorri alle dogliose pene
Il cor mi verrà meno che tu m'a tolto

Unless you succor my grievous pain,
my heart will fail me, which you have taken from me,

7. **(b)** Che la mia vita non sente ma' bene
Se non mirando'l tuo veçoso volto

for my life never feels at ease

unless gazing at your gracious face.

8. **(a)** Da poi fanciulla che d'amor m'a involto
Priego ch'alquanto amɛ beningnia sia.

Since, girl, you have wrapped me in love,
I pray you may be a bit kind to me.

9. **(A)** *Questa fanciull' amor . . .*

This girl, Love . . .

68

Medee fu

Ballade in Manneristic Style

de son pe-re bus - sa,   3. Dont   el - le   fu hi-re-

tie - re   Ne se cu - ra d'es - tre

en roy - al cha - - ie - - re,

Ne   bien   mon - dain a-

1. Medee fu en amer veritable,
   Bien a paru quant Jason enama

   De cuer si vray, si ferme, et si
   estable,
   Que la terre de son pere bussa,

   Dont elle fu hiretiere
   Ne se cura d'estre en royal
   chaiere,
   Ne bien mondain avoir fors son
   amy.
   Ma dame n'a pas ainsy fait a my.

2. Car au premier la trouvay
   [bien] aimable
   Et son ami doucement me
   clama
   Et sanz rayson a esté variable

   Si que s'amour a autre doné ha.

   Ce n'est pas bone maniere
   Quar vraye amour doit estre si
   entiere
   Que ne se doit changier journe
   de mi.
   Ma dame n'a pas ainsy fait a my.

3. Si m'est avis qu'elle est desray-
   sonable
   Autant ou plus que fu Briseÿda.

   Qui en amours eut le cuer si
   amable
   Que sa vie loyauté engarda.

   Helaine a la belle chiere
   N'eut vers Paris par amour
   logiere
   Car vist l'ama et pour s'amour
   gemy.
   Ma dame n'a pas ainsy fait a my.

Medea was true in loving;
   it appeared clearly when she loved
   Jason
with a heart so true, so firm, and
   so immovable
that she abandoned the land of her
   father,
of which she was the heiress.
She was concerned neither to be
   on the royal throne
nor to have worldly goods other
   than her friend.
My lady has not behaved thus to me.

For at first I found her very amiable,
and she sweetly called me her
   friend;
and without cause she has been
   changeable,
so that she has given her love to
   another.
This is not good behavior,
for true love should be so entire

that it would never turn itself
   from me.
My lady has not behaved thus to me.

So I believe that she is unreason-
   able,
as much or more than was Bri-
   seyda,
who in loving had so amiable a
   heart
that she maintained loyalty
   throughout her life.
Helen of the beautiful face
was not lightly in love with Paris,

for she loved him immediately
   and suffered for her love.
My lady has not behaved thus to me.

69

JACOB SENLECHES, *La Harpe de melodie*

Virelai

Ch, fol. 43v, and *Chic* (facsimile on jacket of this book).

1. *The harp of melody, made without melancholy for pleasure, should greatly delight everyone to hear its harmony sound and to see.*

2. And therefore, I agree, for the gracious entertainment of its sweet sound,

3. to compose without any discord in it a chanson of good sentiments

4. to please a company, to have joyous pleasure in seeing me, to flee from unpleasantness, which too much annoys those who take pleasure in hearing

5. *The harp of melody . . .*

The following rondeau, written on the ribbon wound around the post of the harp, gives instructions for performing the unusual notation and the canon in the upper voices. The translation rearranges phrases and lines in an attempt to make these instructions as clear as possible in English.

Se tu me veulz proprement pronuncier	*If you would perform me properly,*
Sus la tenur pour miex estre d'acort	*you should begin a fifth above the tenor*
Diapenthe te convient comencier,	*to be in better accord,*
Ou autrement tu seras en discort.	*or otherwise you will be in discord.*
Pars blanc et noir per mi sans oublier	Let the black and white parts (notes) sound by half,
Lay le tonant, ou tu li feras tort.	without forgetting, or you will do them wrong.
Se tu me veulz proprement pronuncier	*If you would perform me properly*
Sus la tenur pour miex estre d'acort	*above the tenor to be in better accord,*
Puis va cassant duz temps sanz forvoier,	Then follow (chasing) at two units of tempus, without straying;
Premiere note en .d. prent son ressort;	the first note takes its spring from d;

Harpe toudis sans espasse blechier,	harp always without touching (wounding) the spaces;
Par sentement me puis douner confort.	with feeling you can give me comfort (satisfaction).
Se tu me veulz . . . [complete refrain]	*If you would perform me . . .*

As a result of scribal errors in *Ch,* the first section of this virelai has been incorrectly transcribed in the two previously published editions: W. Apel, *French Secular Compositions,* I, No. 92; and N. Josephson, "Vier Beispiele der Ars subtilior," *Archiv für Musikwissenschaft,* XVII (1970), 54–55. The present transcription follows the obviously correct notation in *Chic* (see jacket of this book). Apel's version also ignores the clear indications in *Chic* of first and second endings for the second section. As is often the case, however, these indications fail to show how much of the first ending is to be replaced by the second. Solutions other than the one offered here are therefore possible.

70

JOHANNES CICONIA, *Con lagrime bagnando me*

Ballata

Paris, Bibl. Nat., ital. 568, fols. 52v–53.

1. *With tears bathing my face I have left my lord, wherefore I languish in woe when I see myself abandoned [separated from him in tenor].*

2. O my suffering! O harsh separation! That you will never return in this world.

3. O crude death! O pitiless life! How you have dissolved my joyous love.

4. Ah, greedy bottomless wickedness, beyond all soothing, break henceforth your scale, for you have taken away all my joy and laughter.

5. *With tears . . .*

71

COOKE, *Stella celi*

Prayer to the Virgin Mary in English Descant

Stel - la   ce - li   ex - tir - pa - - vit

Que la -cta- vit   Do - mi - - num   Mor - tis   pe - stem

quam plan - ta - vit   Pri - mus   pa - rens ho - mi - - num:

Old Hall Manuscript, now in the British Library (formerly the British Museum), add. MS 57950, fol. 40v.

I - psa stel - la nunc di - gne - tur Si - de - ra com-pe - sce - re

Quo-rum bel - la ple -- bem ce-dunt Di - re mor-tis ul - ce - re.

Star of heaven who suckled the Lord and rooted out the plague of death that
the first parent of mankind planted; may the same star now deign to curb
the constellations whose wars are killing people by the sore of dreadful
death.

---

* Coloration in m. 9 and the triple division of the semibreve (♩) in mm. 9 and 18
show that the mensuration in the first half of this antiphon is imperfect time and perfect prolation. The breve of the first half ( ) should therefore equal the breve in
perfect time and minor prolation ( ), which is indicated in the manuscript by a
circle in all voices.